THE CAMPUS AND THE MICROCOMPUTER REVOLUTION

THE CAMPUS AND THE MICROCOMPUTER REVOLUTION

PRACTICAL ADVICE FOR NONTECHNICAL DECISION MAKERS

J. Victor Baldridge
Janine Woodward Roberts
Terri A. Weiner

American Council on Education • Macmillan Publishing Company
NEW YORK

Collier Macmillan Publishers
LONDON

Macmillan Publishing Company
A Division of Macmillan, Inc.
866 Third Avenue, New York, N.Y. 10022

Collier Macmillan Canada, Inc.

Library of Congress Catalog Card Number: 84-2834

Printed in the United States of America

printing number
1 2 3 4 5 6 7 8 9 10

Library of Congress Cataloging in Publication Data

Baldridge, J. Victor
  The campus and the microcomputer revolution.

  (The American Council on Education/Macmillan series in
higher education)
  Bibliography: p.
  Includes index.
    1. Universities and colleges—Data processing.
2. Universities and colleges—Computer programs—Purchas-
ing. I. Roberts, Janine Woodward. II. Weiner, Terri A.
III. Title. IV. Series.
LB2324.B33 1984   378'.0028'54   84-2834
ISBN 0-02-901370-4

Permission to reprint the following material is gratefully acknowledged:
        Charles Farrell, "The Computerization of Carnegie-Mellon." *The Chronicle of
            Higher Education,* March 30, 1983.
        SIGI Information Bulletin. Educational Testing Service, Princeton, New Jersey.

CONTENTS

PREFACE

A computer revolution is sweeping through American higher education. At the cutting edge is the microcomputer, that remarkable technological breakthrough that is revolutionizing business, science, government, and, yes, even education. In education, there is much excitement, a feeling that this is the threshold of genuine educational innovation. But there is also much confusion. A bewildering, buzzing disarray of decisions must be made: resources must be redirected, programs must be reshaped, retraining efforts must be mounted.

This book is about three things: the *microcomputers,* the *institutions* that will be using them, and the *decisions* that will link them. You should understand the scope of the book so that your expectations and the book's intentions are well matched.

KEY THEMES IN THE BOOK

First, the book focuses on *microcomputers,* not on larger machines. Of course, the larger machines will continue to exist, and a key issue of the future will be *linkage* between microcomputers and larger computers. But you should not depend on this book for advice about larger computers.

Second, the book discusses the use of computers in the *instructional program,* in the *general curriculum,* and in *administration.* Other areas such as research uses and office automation are important, but the book addresses them only briefly. The spotlight is heavily on curricular and, to a lesser degree, administrative uses.

Third, the book is *practical* and *decision-oriented.* If you are looking for research on the effectiveness of computers or some other topic, this is not the right place. We will be talking about practical matters—selecting curriculum focal points, setting up labs, buying machines and software, developing training programs for personnel. This book will give you solid, practical advice on many issues:

- What are appropriate *goals* for a campus-wide computer literacy program?
- How can competing demands between the traditional *mainframe advocates* and the new *microcomputer advocates* be balanced?
- If the campus had limited expansion funds, what should the *growth pattern* look like?
- If the campus decides to install microcomputers, what *configuration* makes the most sense?
- What are reasonable *criteria* for judging microcomputers and how does one select among competing brands?
- What *educational software* is available and how does one get it?
- How much *faculty retraining* is needed and how does one obtain it?
- What *curriculum adaptations* are needed for a computer literacy program?

THE DECISION DYNAMICS ABOUT COMPUTERS

The book speaks to practicing administrators, faculty, and trustees who have decisions to make, money to allocate, disputes to settle, and competing demands to balance. The book's purpose is not to make the decisions for you but to give some additional information to help weight the alternatives.

What about the role of "experts" in the decision process? Computers are a bewildering business. They come in all shapes and sizes, the terminology is like Greek to most, and the computer Priesthood seems to speak a foreign language as well. It is difficult for a nontechnical administrator to comprehend this bewildering array of computer jargon. There is a prevailing temptation to call in the experts, stand back from the fray, and pray for the best. This "turn-it-over-to-the-experts" attitude is shortsighted and totally unnecessary.

We have watched too many forceful administrators suddenly become intimidated when confronted with large-scale computer decisions. A baseline idea needs to be established. The key policymakers, even though nontechnical, are nevertheless experts about the *decision arena*. Fundamentally that is what we confront here: a decision arena focused on computers. The nontechnical decision makers—administrators, faculty committee members, trustees, department heads—are experts about many issues:

- The overall shape of the *curriculum* on your campus and how computer literacy fits into the whole.

○ The *political dynamics* of your campus, the competing interest groups who are going to fight over computer resources, and the history of previous battles.

○ The *administration computing requirements* and how they fit into the puzzle. The available *resource capabilities* and how they can be allocated among various campus needs.

○ The *expertise* across your campus that can be harnessed into a synergistic whole.

In short, the nontechnical policymaker is nevertheless an expert on a range of critical issues. The nontechnical administrator should never be buffaloed by the esoteric vocabulary and the endless jargon of the computer expert. Thinking administrators know they have a vital contribution to make. They will be bold about making those contributions.

On the other hand, this is no excuse for pigheadedness. There *are* technical issues at stake and the computer experts *do* know their side of the equation. Although the nontechnical person should never be cowed by the experts, a little modesty really is in order. Patient listening makes eminent sense. So you, the nontechnical decisionmaker, bring a special expertise to the table; the computer experts also bring important knowledge. A dynamic mix is needed: *management* expertise on one side and *computer* expertise on the other. This mixture, salted liberally with other expert opinions from all over the campus, can produce an effective campus program.

RESEARCH AND EXPERIENCE BEHIND THIS BOOK

This book is based on years of research and experience dealing with management issues, campus policies, and computers. In the early 1970s the Exxon Education Foundation began a program called the Resource Allocation and Management Program (RAMP). RAMP's purpose was to improve college management in liberal arts colleges throughout the United States. By that time many large colleges had already installed computers for their administrative purposes, but most small institutions did not have administrative computing facilities. Most colleges in the program chose to install minicomputers and to develop a Management Information System (MIS).

In order to determine the success of their management-improvement program, the Exxon Education Foundation funded a large evaluation project, conducted by the Higher Education Research Institute at the University of California, Los Angeles (UCLA). For over five years a research team from our staff studied the forty-nine private colleges that introduced management information systems. The senior author of this book was one leader in that research team and, based on that research, published the book *New Patterns of Management* (Baldridge and Tierney, 1979). One key purpose of that book was to examine the strengths and weaknesses of computers in college management. That project formed the cornerstone for nearly a decade of our research about improving college management, often examining computers both in administration and in the curriculum.

After the Exxon evaluation project was completed, the Higher Education Research Institute in 1981 formed a consortium of eight Southern California liberal arts colleges. Again the purpose was to improve college management, this time with an eye to reducing student attrition. The campuses were concerned about several computer issues: administrative computing, student data, management information systems, and faculty training in computers. As a consequence, the eight campuses installed many microcomputers and a training program was developed.

From that consortium effort a substantial program was spawned concerning the use of microcomputers in colleges, both in administration and in the curriculum. In late 1982, the Higher Education Research Institute at UCLA decided to establish a program called Computer Horizons: A Project to Enhance Computer Competencies on Campus. The senior author of this book was named coordinator. The Horizons Project, located in the Graduate School of Education, started programs to promote microcomputer training, installation, and curriculum developments on campuses. Workshops and training sessions were held for administrators on a regional basis, with over 400 administrators participating in the program in the first year. In addition, staff from the Horizons Project frequently served as consultants to colleges that were installing campus-wide programs in computer literacy.

In short, this book depends on a decade of research and action concerning the use of computers in college management, in particular on the experience of the last two years working with microcomputer programs. A significant portion of this book was developed in the field, working with colleges on campus-wide microcomputer literacy programs.

ACKNOWLEDGMENTS

In writing a book, many hard-working people are involved in one way or another. We are extremely grateful to those who have contributed to the production of this book. The many individuals who have participated in our microcomputer workshops and seminars have given us insight into the varying needs of the college administrator. The ideas and knowledge they have shared have been incorporated into this book. The computer companies have also been very generous with interviews and technical information.

There are several individuals who deserve special recognition and thanks for the time and energy spent in assisting us. All of the following are involved in some way with academic administration or computing, and their comments and critiques were vital to the production of this book. Ted Marchese and Lou Alpert from the American Association for Higher Education both did prepublication reviews. An in-depth analysis was provided by Richard D. Breslin, vice-president for academic affairs at Iona College. Kenneth C. Green of the Higher Education Research Institute at UCLA, with his extensive knowledge and background in academic computing, spent considerable time reviewing the manuscript, and his help was important. Other reviewers were: Michael Donnelan, vice-president of the College of Notre Dame; Daryl G. Smith, vice-president for planning and research at Scripps College; Robert Birnbaum, professor of higher education at Columbia University; George Ecker from the school of education at Ohio State University; Billy E. Frye, vice-president and chief administrative officer; Charles Thomas, president of CAUSE. Hans H. Jenny, executive vice-president of Chapman College, has contributed various charts in addition to an extensive review of the first half of the manuscript. Kevin Roberts assisted us with his knowledge of interactive video and wrote that section of the book. And finally, thanks to our secretary, Judy Hirahara, who put many hours of hard work into getting the text on paper.

A NOTE ABOUT OUR RELATIONSHIP TO DIGITAL EQUIPMENT COMPANY

The manuscript was finished and mailed to the publishers for editing when a very pleasant surprise occurred: the Digital Equipment Company (DEC) made a substantial grant in support of the Computer Horizons Project being established by the Higher Education Research Institute in the Graduate School of Education at UCLA.

This relationship needs to be clearly specified, and we need to underscore our position about DEC products. Our manuscript said good things about DEC microcomputers—as it did about IBM, Apple, and Hewlett Packard. But we said those things *before* we were involved with DEC, and no substantial changes were made to the manuscript after we learned of the DEC grant to UCLA.

In short, we are pleased and excited about DEC's support of our UCLA programs. But our high opinion of DEC was formed well beforehand, and was committed to paper in this manuscript long before the grant was obtained. DEC personnel had not seen the manuscript before they made the grant; after they saw it, they sighed with relief!

THE CAMPUS AND
THE MICROCOMPUTER
REVOLUTION

CHAPTER 1

THE COMPUTER REVOLUTION

ARRIVES ON CAMPUS

The high technology revolution has been moving through American society for the past twenty years. For example, Porat (1977) describes the shift in our economy from agriculture to industry to information processing activities, which—broadly defined—now accounts for almost half of the gross national product.

The revolution has arrived on the campuses. The new technologies take a bewildering number of forms, applications, and hardware. Television is making a great impact in many "open university" settings; cable television is opening up entirely new educational markets flung as far as the wires and the big dishes transmit signals; electronic mail zips messages from one user to another; huge national research bases and information networks are available at the touch of the keyboard. At the heart of this electronic revolution stands the computer—the brains and lightning-like reflexes that support the electronic society.

THEMES IN THE COMPUTER REVOLUTION

Here is a potpourri of facts about the high tech revolution that is driven by the computer's almost limitless brain.

Almost Every Man, Woman, and Child in the United States Has "Indirect" Contact with a Computer Every Day

Every person at some point in the day interacts with another person who is working directly with a computer. The computer is only one person-link away from every one of us, even if we do not work on the computer ourselves. When you buy groceries the transaction is probably tallied by a computer; when you withdraw money from the bank the teller is probably working on a computer; when you make plane reservations the agent books your flight with a computer; when you make telephone

1

calls across the country computers route the lightning-fast signals and bounce them around a satellite; when you have your car serviced the engine performance is probably assessed by a computer's blinking lights; when your paycheck is processed by your organization's payroll office the dollar signs are stamped by a computer. The teacher in the classroom, the astronaut circling overhead, the president of the United States, the worker assembling boxes on the assembly line—they all share the common human fate that they are never more than one person-link away from a computer, and those linkages occur almost every day of their lives.

Within Ten to Fifteen Years Virtually Every Person Will Have "Direct" Dealings with a Computer Every Day

According to Morgan Lewis, senior research specialist with the National Center for Research in Vocational Education, by the year 2000 "some ability to work with the various electronic devices will be basic, whether that person is in sales or medicine." No, every person will *not* have to be a programmer, nor will the interaction be through the familiar computer keyboard. Nevertheless, every person will probably directly operate a computer within ten to fifteen years. The computer will not require the user to be a programmer, because it will work with voice-activated commands, with touch screens that allow you to draw with your fingertips, with simple "menus" of activities that even a child could perform.

Operating a computer will be only a bit more difficult than operating today's telephone. Every person will probably use a computer almost every single day. By 1995 every home in the United States, with a few rare exceptions, will have some type of home computer. Such a suggestion would have been called outrageous ten years ago. But you, the reader, are likely to greet it with only a yawn. Our expectations change very rapidly and it no longer seems absurd that every family will have a computer tomorrow just as they have a television today.

What will those ever present blinking little brains do? Well, almost anything you can imagine: allow you to work at home, pay the monthly bills, shop from electronic catalogs, figure your income taxes, connect you to a worldwide electronic mail network, run your sophisticated household electronic system, do your word processing, or link you to the worldwide video encyclopedia that is already under development at the Atari Institute. In short, the computer's versatility and usefulness will be limited primarily by your imagination, personal knowledge, and human needs—not by the computer's limitations.

The Cost of Computing Power Is Dropping Dramatically

The multimillion dollar computers that filled up four-story buildings twenty years ago can now sit on your desk, at a price equal to one month's executive pay. According to John McCredie, president of EDUCOM, the price of computer hardware at a comparable level has been declining at a yearly rate of approximately 25 percent for the past ten years (1983). That means, for instance, that a specified task that cost $200,000 ten years ago probably costs only $11,263 today! Hardware is becoming so inexpensive that it is usually much smarter to junk an old piece of computer equipment and buy a new one rather than trying to upgrade the old.

Recently the University of California paid a demolition company to dispose of a computer that, less than a decade ago, cost over $10 million. Computers and their associated software are dropping so dramatically in price that they are, by themselves, a major productivity factor in the entire national economy. To illustrate this point, a Rolls Royce automobile that cost roughly $50,000 in 1975 would cost only $5,600 today if automobile productivity was going up as fast as computer productivity. In fact that Rolls Royce will cost you about $145,000 today!

In spite of dropping hardware costs, colleges must be alert to other computer costs that are *increasing* rapidly. Some expenses associated *with* computers have been rising almost as dramatically as Rolls Royce costs—personnel costs to run them and to design software, for example. EDUCOM'S McCreadie points out that the cost of support personnel for computers will increase by 75 percent in the next few years. In addition, staffing computer personnel will be exacerbated by the extreme shortage of graduates in computer-related fields. Consequently, in addition to being more expensive, information processing professionals will also become harder to recruit and retain. (We will discuss this aspect of cost later in the book.)

New Computer Based Technologies Are Emerging Every Day

The only thing really predictable about the future is its unpredictability. We can, however, venture some guesses that will probably be much too conservative. *Guess one:* Truly powerful computers will be developed to fit in your coat pocket and go to work with you. *Guess two:* The primitive "electronic mail" links of today will be as sophisticated as your telephone within this decade. *Guess three:* Massive research and information libraries will be at the finger tips of every citizen in the country within the decade. *Guess four:* By the end of the decade, every child in the United States will be computer literate at some minimal level by the time he or she is eight years old. *Guess five:* By 1995 at least 50 percent of the jobs in the United States will require an active working knowledge of computers. *Guess six:* In 1995 almost every course in every college and university will use computers to some extent.

The Computer Revolution Is More Than a Passing Fad

At our training workshops for campuses someone always asks the question: "Isn't all this emphasis on computers just a passing fad? I remember when audio-visuals were going to revolutionize education, too, but now they gather dust."

We doubt that computers are a passing fad. The proper analogy is not with audio-visual equipment; the correct comparison is with the telephone. Try running today's society without phones, and you will know how it will be to run tomorrow's world without computers! We believe the impact on the college curriculum will be just as substantial, and we predict significant computer usage throughout the whole range of subject-matter fields. The box on page 5 has examples of how some campuses are becoming part of the revolution.

PHASES IN COMPUTER USAGE: THE MICROCOMPUTER IS THE LEADER

The current revolution in the computing world focuses on the microcomputer, those little desktop computers that are becoming so familiar. In terms of sheer expansion of computer power, user base, and public computer literacy the microcomputer is clearly the driving force behind the current computing revolution. Because of the radical cost reductions that microcomputers furnish, they provide a great democratizing element in the computer industry. Now every family in America is potentially a computer user.

Any sensible person could divide the history of computing into many stages, but for our purposes four stages seem important. Each stage still exists, with the older stages standing along side the newer.

Stage One: Batch Processing

Stage one was the era of the large computer, housed in a central location, and operated through *batch* processing. Batch processing required the user to go to the computer, to place data into card reading machines, wait in line for the outcome, and then go to a central location to pick up the printout. The wait might be hours or even days; and after waiting, the hapless user might find that a tiny mistake in the beginning of the program had ruined the process. Moreover, the cost was exceedingly high—even if the output was worthless!

Stage Two: Time-Sharing

Stage two was the era of *time-sharing*. Time-sharing was a dramatic step up from batch processing in terms of user convenience. Now users were able to access the computer through decentralized terminals. Users sat at the terminal and entered information that was then processed by the central computer. Things were considerably more convenient under time-sharing. Users could work from their own location and the time lags were reduced between data entry and output. Nevertheless, time-sharing still

---

REQUIRED OR PROVIDED, MICROCOMPUTERS PROLIFERATE ON CAMPUSES

Drexel University
Philadelphia, Pennsylvania
> Freshman are required to buy McIntosh microcomputers by Apple for $1,000. Faculty and upperclassmen will also be entitled to buy.

Brown University
Providence, Rhode Island
> All students and faculty will be provided with a personal computer "workstation." Discounts and financial aid will be available if personal purchasing is desired.

Clarkson College
Potsdam, New York
> Fall 1983 freshmen will be furnished with a Zenith Z-100 desktop computer—retail value $4,000—yet students will be charged only $200 per semester. Eight semesters later, students will own their microcomputer.

Stevens Institute of Technology
Hoboken, New Jersey
> Students are required to buy Digital Equipment Corporation's Professional 325 personal computers @ $1,800. (Price is after a subsidy from Stevens and an educational discount from Digital.)

University of Colorado
Boulder, Colorado
> By law, the university is unable to sell computers to faculty members. Nevertheless, faculty can use microcomputers under users fee amounting to one-third of retail cost.

Western New England College
Springfield, Massachusetts
> A payroll deduction plan is offered—the purchase price of the microcomputer is deducted from each paycheck for three years. After three years the computer can be bought for one dollar.

Chapman College
Orange, California
> A payroll deduction plan for computers is offered to faculty members over the course of one year (after a discount from Apple).

---

required a central computer to do the work, a wait in line until the product could be executed, and a trip to a central output facility to get the printout. Although it was more convenient, the umbilical cord still ran from the mother computer to the baby terminal—and the mother computer still controlled everything.

Stage Three: Decentralized, Real-Time Computing

Stage three is the arrival of the *microcomputer*, and a shift to "real time." Unlike the previous two stages the users now have their *own* computers and they do exactly what the users want them to do. The microcomputer works in "real time," responding instantaneously to whatever the user is entering. There is no wait between what the user wants to do and what the computer does because that computer is working only for this single user. The convenience of the microcomputer is amazing considering the inconvenience of batch processing, and the only somewhat better inconveniences of time-sharing. In fact, if every microcomputer were powerful enough to do all jobs a user ever needed, there would be no need for big mainframe computers. Instead every user would have a completely adequate microcomputer. But that is the rub—every microcomputer does not have the power to service the user's every need. This leads us into the future, into stage four.

Stage Four: Networking

Networking is the heart of stage four. Since every microcomputer lacks the full power needed by every user it will be necessary to maintain extremely large computers in centralized locations for specialized tasks, and then link up those large computers with microcomputers in decentralized locations. For most users most of the time, the microcomputer is quite adequate for most jobs. But the microcomputer cannot handle some tasks: extremely large data-crunching tasks, heavy-duty filing activities with great numbers of cases, super graphics that require highly specialized equipment, and large-scale scientific programming. Because we continue to need the sheer *power* of large computers, and because we all want the sheer *convenience* of small microcomputers, we are driven toward networking.

The microcomputer, then, is the spearhead of the new "network" computer systems of the future. Currently there is much talk about networking microcomputers but very little action on the promises. Nevertheless, in the next few years the technology will be fully developed and we will see the widespread use of microcomputers and larger computers linked in networks. Later in the book, networking will be discussed in greater detail.

ACADEMIC APPLICATIONS OF COMPUTING

A campus has many uses for computers. Again, you can divide the cake in about as many different ways as the cake cutter would like. For our purposes a crude division into four usage categories will be sufficient: (1) administrative applications; (2) scientific and research uses; (3) computer assisted instruction; and (4) office automation.

Administrative Applications

Large university campus administrative applications generally absorb 50 to 60 percent of the computing usage. These activities cover a broad spectrum, including accounting, physical plant scheduling, payroll, student registration, registrar's records, budgeting analysis, and personnel files. On many campuses the heavy strain caused by huge administrative usage often causes problems with academic usage. Larger campuses tend to separate the functions so that there is a dedicated computer for administrative applications and a separate computing facility for academic usage.

Scientific and Research Applications

Campuses with large computing capability find that faculty research and scientific applications will typically consume about 20 percent of the computer usage. Although there may be some student instruction intermingled with these activities, the main purpose is for scholarly work of the faculty themselves. The accompanying instruction is likely to be strictly at the graduate level. Examples of this application are large-scale statistical analyses by social scientists, complex programming efforts by natural scientists, and a broad spectrum of grants and contracts work for outside agencies.

Computer-Assisted Instruction

A very small proportion of the computing power on every campus is dedicated to computer-assisted instruction, probably 10 to 20 percent depending on the size of the computer science department in the institution. Computer-assisted instructions can basically be broken into two parts. First, there is instruction about the computer itself in computer science departments and in computer literacy programs. Second, there is the use of the computer in other direct instruction. The development of large computer-assisted instruction (CAI) packages such as PLATO and CAN has expanded computerized instructions in areas other than computer science. Today a student can take over 10,000 hours of PLATO lessons, including a wide spectrum of the humanities, social sciences, and natural sciences. Most of this computer-assisted instruction is available only on large computers. But some instructional packages have been reconfigured, and in the near future microcomputers will be widely used in this enterprise.

Office Automation

Finally, computers are used in offices. Word processing is the backbone of office automation on every campus. But office automation can also include electronic filing, electronic mail, linkage to national data bases and resource catalogues, and a number of other activities. It is quite surprising that colleges and universities have invested very little computer capacity in office automation up to this point. Word processing is just barely making a toehold on most campuses and more sophisticated office automation activities are rarely found. It is still a rare campus that has a serious electronic mail network. Typically, not even 1 percent of a campus computing budget is devoted to office automation matters. Nevertheless, the future outlook for office automation on campuses is bright as productivity is demonstrated and prices continue to fall.

COMPUTER USERS ON THE CAMPUS

The campus breaks down into various user groups that sometimes seem to have the intensity of religious camps; some worship the god of the computer but others fight it. Different people have different stances and their attitudes will help determine how computers are used, whether they are readily accepted or deeply opposed. Let us examine the five "religious" computer sects.

The Priesthood

The priesthood controls the computers and develops computer science. The computer science professors and the directors of computer centers have scientific knowledge about computers and actually run the computer establishments on the campus. Of course, the priesthood is the most important advocate group for computing. In the past some members of the priesthood have worried that the microcomputer's arrival would undermine their empires, allowing the common people to have direct access to the god. Today, however, most members of the priesthood have converted, embracing microcomputers (coupled with networking to larger computers) as the wave of the future.

The True Believers

The true believers are heavy computer users: the scientists, social scientists, and administrative users who have traditionally employed computers in their work. Although they are not computer scientists they are nevertheless savvy about computing and use it regularly. In the past the true believers advocated large computers, since they cut their professional teeth on these machines. They are the natural allies of the priesthood; in the past they rarely advocated microcomputers since their experience was with larger computers. Many true believers, however, are developing a love for microcomputers—joining the ranks of the new converts.

The New Converts

New converts are people who have recently started using computers. They are usually fans of the microcomputer—the social scientists, humanists, and administrators who have discovered that microcomputers can do important tasks for them. Many new converts were occasional users of large mainframes, but it took the microcomputer to really set them on fire. New converts often have a missionary zeal. They are anxious to convert other people to the new gospel!

The Skeptics

Another large segment of the campus are the skeptics. The skeptics neither favor nor oppose computers. They simply don't know what all the fuss is about. They suspect this fad, like hula hoops and supply-side economics, will soon pass. These are the humanists and the other noncomputer users. They are not strongly opposed to computing and sometimes they even have a mild interest. But basically they are not interested in this development, suspect it is a passing fad, and have a wait-and-see attitude.

The Antagonists

The antagonists are not neutral like the skeptics; they are actively opposed to the spread of computers on the campus. The antagonists are probably a small group, since most people are content to play skeptic if they do not favor computers. But the antagonists can be a very vocal and aggressive group, fighting against budget allocations for computers, and actively working to stop the introduction of computers into the curriculum.

The antagonists have a number of important concerns. First, they worry about the impersonality and depersonalization that computers may bring. Second, they fear computers are a passing phenomenon that will absorb scarce financial resources that could be better allocated. Third, they fret that computers might threaten faculty and staff jobs in the cirriculum and in the office. In sum, the antagonists have many worries and they aggressively voice their opposition. Table 1-1 briefly describes campus users.

TABLE 1-1. CAMPUS USERS

Priesthood:	Computer center directors and computer science experts.
True believers:	Heavy scientific and administrative users of mainframe computers.
New converts:	New users, usually strong advocates of microcomputers.
Skeptics:	Not pro or con, simply don't care and don't know what all the fuss is about.
Antagonists:	Opposition based on fears of depersonalization and misallocation of scarce resources.

CAMPUS USER GROUPS AND CAMPUS POLITICS

How big are these groups on the campus? This varies by campus and at best we offer some crude guesses. On the average campus the priesthood is probably less than 5 percent of the faculty and staff, the true believers are probably about 15 percent, the new converts are another 20 percent, the skeptics are about 35 percent, and the antagonists are roughly 25 percent. Naturally, the breakdown varies dramatically by institution. These percentages probably apply to the typical liberal arts college, while a technical institute or research university would have fewer skeptics and fewer antagonists.

What difference does all this make? Why does it matter that the campus is broken into these user groups? The answer is politics. The campus, like the rest of the human world, is splintered into interest groups who want to claim the resource pie. These computer religions are fighting over resource priorities, budgets, space, equipment, and curriculum issues.

The Political Battles

The first political battle is between the computer advocates (priesthood, true believers, and new converts) and the rest of the campus (skeptics and antagonists). Computer advocates, of course, want more money for computing, while the rest of the campus may not see the urgency and may even oppose it. The mix of these different groups in the faculty and in the administration will determine whether a campus makes progress toward a major use of computers.

In the recent past, the second political fight was often between the priesthood and the true believers on the one hand, and the new converts on the other. The priesthood and their allies were likely to emphasize large computers, while the new converts wanted to put more resources into microcomputers. Sometimes the fights *within* a computer advocate camp were more vicious than the fights between the users and the non-users. The history of the human race repeats itself again: fights among the believers are usually as vicious as fights against the nonbelievers. On the whole, however, this second political war has diminished as more and more priesthood members embrace the microcomputer revolution.

The Decision Maker's Dilemma

The decision maker, then, faces a splintered campus. Major campus groups will not support any expansion of computer usage, will actively oppose it, and will argue that scarce resources should not go to this passing fad. Then the decision maker might face a second battle—among the computer believers there can be war between the different sects about the best approach to computing. Administrators will be pushed and pulled in all directions. Unfortunately, as soon as they make a decision all the other groups will scream bloody murder! It's the classic case of damned-if-you-do-and-damned-if-you-don't.

The arguments between the believers and the nonbelievers are simple—computer advocates want more money, and the nonbelievers want to use it elsewhere. The old arguments *within* the computer camp were usually more perplexing to the decision maker. The priesthood and the true believers were demanding more money for traditional computing patterns, for mainframe computers, for departmental computer budgets, for additional computer center staff. By contrast, the new converts were arguing for microcomputers and for new computer budgets where they previously never existed. These, then, are the political dimensions of the computer decision process. And although the level of contention is gradually declining as microcomputers are widely accepted, decision makers will still sometimes be caught in its whirlpool.

The Bias of This Book

Our prejudices, obvious all through the book, are the following:

1. *Campuses should, and will, expand their computing activities.* The antagonist's fears sometimes may be legitimate. But on the whole we feel that computing is here to stay and will expand dramatically in the foreseeable future.

2. *Central computing facilities will of course continue for specialized purposes.* But we also anticipate that most rapid growth will occur through *distributed* systems. The microcomputer will be the lead development in distributed systems, and networking between microcomputers and larger computers will become increasingly common.

3. *What about the political wars between the priesthood and the new converts?* On most campuses this war was over by the fall of 1983 when EDUCOM met at Stanford. By and large the priesthood had been converted and had joined forces with the new converts. Nevertheless, on some campuses this battle still must be fought. In those situations we believe that the decision makers ought to favor the new converts for the immediate future. The priesthood is too well entrenched and has too many vested interests to be impartial judges of how computing should develop. War is too important to be left to the generals; campus computing is too essential to be left to the "experts" in the priesthood. We believe microcomputers should be spread widely on the campus and be given full support, even in those increasingly rare cases where the priesthood opposes it. In the future this battle will end, because microcomputers *will* be widespread. For the immediate future, however, administrators should lean in the direction of the Martin Luther Solution—give microcomputers to the people and let them decide how to handle their own religion!

WHAT'S GOING ON?

A study by EDUCOM (McCredie, 1983) examined the strategies used by ten different innovative and progressive colleges and universities in the information processing area. According to the EDUCOM staff, the strategy taken by a particular institution will primarily depend on its existing academic character and management style. Nevertheless, EDUCOM found several common fundamental elements in the strategies used by these ten colleges:

1. *Organizational Structure:* Eight of the ten institutions had a single individual or administrative office to coordinate computer-related issues.
2. *Decentralization:* All institutions are moving toward more decentralized computer facilities.
3. *Personal Computers:* All the institutions are actively encouraging innovative uses of personal computer systems.
4. *Networking:* All ten organizations are involved with both local and national networking activities.
5. *Library Automation:* All ten organizations are involved with or planning toward a collaboration between computers and library resources.
6. *Information Processing Literacy:* All ten campuses have assigned task forces to examine the computer literacy question for college graduates.
7. *Text Processing:* Text processing is considered to be an important element to academic computer literacy and administrative support in all institutions.
8. *Electronic Mail:* All of the organizations have either established or are actively considering establishing extensive electronic mail systems to allow informal communication among faculty, students, and administrators.

CHAPTER 2

DEVELOPING A CAMPUS-WIDE

COMPUTER PROGRAM

Campuses all over the country are exploring ways to expand and enrich their computing activities, especially in curriculum efforts. Of course, many institutions already have a rich, long tradition of widespread computer usage in their instructional program. Institutions like Carnegie-Mellon, the Massachusetts Institute of Technology, and the California Institute of Technology have, of course, had systematic computer usage for decades. In fact, most colleges have used computers for years in computer science departments, in data-oriented social science disciplines, in many natural sciences, and for administrative purposes. According to Hamblen and Baird (1979), approximately 90 percent of colleges and universities have access to some form of computing capability. About half of the total academic computer expenditures is for administrative data processing applications.

STEPS IN A CAMPUS-WIDE PROGRAM

In spite of this widespread capacity it seems reasonable to state that on most campuses most of the time most students and faculty do not have much serious exposure to computer usage. We guess that on the majority of campuses 50 percent of the undergraduate students have never touched a computer keyboard, much less learned to use it in their daily activities. Most of American higher education needs to think seriously about computing and about the human interface between students, faculty, staff, administrators, and the machines. This chapter outlines some steps that every campus ought to examine carefully.

Step One: Set Computer Literacy Goals
"Computer literacy" is one of the fuzziest terms floating around these days. As with the terms "democracy" and "truth," almost every-

body has a different idea about what computer literacy means. Several national commissions and task forces have tried to define this elusive term. In early 1983, for example, both the Department of Education's Office of Institutional Research and Improvement and the National Center for Education Statistics announced plans to sponsor studies to develop a working definition of computer literacy in elementary and secondary education. In addition, EDUCOM, a computer consortium of 400 colleges and universities, started a two-part computer literacy study in 1983. The EDUCOM Computer Literacy project will attempt to help higher education overcome three major barriers to achieving effective coherent Computer Literacy Programs:

1. Lack of a widely supported definition and criteria for evaluating present instructional programs and directing the development of new ones.
2. Lack of an effective feedback system for identifying successful computer literacy program models in some institutions and for adapting and disseminating them to others.
3. Confusion caused by the flood of vendor claims about new hardware, software, and "courseware."

The first part of EDUCOM's study will examine present computer *literacy requirements* at colleges and universities throughout the nation. The second part will report on *model programs* of computer literacy. EDUCOM hopes, through these activities, to provide an intellectual framework for computer literacy programs in higher education. For more information on this study contact EDUCOM, P.O. Box 364, Princeton, N.J. 08540.

In the meantime, while these national commissions study the problem, other people have taken the bull by the horns and proposed their own computer literacy goals. Several authors (see Johnson et al., 1980; Klassen et al., 1980) suggest that computer literacy:

1. imparts knowledge about handling information;
2, dispels fears and myths associated with computers;
3. develops skills in using and programming a computer;
4. develops procedural learning;
5. addresses the ethical and societal issues raised by computing.

Campuses have also defined computer literacy for their own purposes. Pepperdine University appointed an Academic Computing Advisory Committee, which stated "that all graduates of Pepperdine University, regardless of school, both graduates and undergraduates, be required to be computer literate as a requirement for graduation." The committee defines computer literacy as having "the ability to write a simple computer program to solve a problem, to understand the basic components of

STAGES IN COMPUTER COMPETENCY*

Computer competency is not easily defined. It does seem, however, that there are stages one goes through in becoming computer competent. The following taxonomy illustrates these. The first three stages are oriented to the general user. The latter three stages would be more appropriate for those interested in the technicalities of computer science and engineering.

Stage One: Basics
The fundamentals are accomplished here: learning how to operate the system; the uses of the system; and the computer's role in society.

Stage Two: Applications Programs
Once a basic understanding of the system is grasped, stage two involves learning to use applications or preprogrammed software such as word processing, budget spreadsheets, or data base management.

Stage Three: Interface Between Applications Programs and Work Environment
Adapting applications software to specific work activities or disciplines is the next logical stage. More than merely learning an application program, this stage focuses on sophisticated understanding of the *interface* between the program and the work environment.

Stage Four: Fundamental Programming
Computer languages and programming skills are the heart of stage four. Of course, within this stage there are various levels of competency, from the very simple to the moderately complex.

Stage Five: Beginning Computer Science
Once languages are understood, the next level is to explore the theory and application of the computer science discipline.

Stage Six: Advanced Computer Science
The final stage in computer competence includes advanced computer programming, software development, and computer design.

*Adapted from personal correspondence with Hans H. Jenny, executive vice-president, Chapman College, Orange, California.

a computer, and to demonstrate abilities to utilize software packages, including word processing."

Benjamin Mittman (1983), professor of computer science and the director of the Academic Computing Center at Northwestern University, feels very strongly about implementing computer literacy programs in the college curriculum. The primary goal of a computer literacy course, Mittman argues, should be to *understand* computers, what they can and cannot do, and communicate to the students and faculties the roles of computers in their lives. Incidentally, Mittman also insists that computer literacy in colleges should not be an either/or situation. Students should not be forced to choose between foreign language and computer literacy—both subjects should be incorporated into the field of study.

Each college or university embarking on a computer enhancement program will have to debate its goals and its definitions of computer literacy or computer competency. Of course, the faculty will have to be heavily involved in the process. Sometimes the debate may be difficult and noisy—but the debate must occur and must be resolved.

Step Two: Assess the Current State of Instructional Computing on Your Campus

Very few colleges are starting from scratch. Most campuses have some history of computer use. The first move is to determine the current state of affairs. A campus Task Force on Computing should be established to answer the following questions about *instructional* use of computers.

1. What *departments* currently are heavy computer users in their curriculum? How do they use them?
2. What are the *general education requirements,* if any, regarding computers?
3. What *computer-assisted instruction* (CAI) is currently used on the campus's large computers? Have they been expanded lately? Have they been evaluated recently?
4. Are there separate *academic* and *administrative* computing facilities? What is the pattern? What have been the strengths and weaknesses of the arrangements?
5. Who controls *budget allocations* for computing? Is that procedure adequate?
6. What *microcomputers* are used on campuses? By whom, for what, to what extent? Is there a policy regarding microcomputer purchases?
7. What microcomputer *laboratories* exist? How are they used?
8. Are there microcomputer *purchase plans* for employees, faculty, and students? How effective are they?

Incidentally, may we be so bold as to suggest that members of the Task Force read this book *before* they answer those questions for your campus!

Step Three: Plan for Widespread Access to Computer Facilities

It is impossible to have a computer literacy program without widespread access to computers. Unfortunately this usually means spending money—lots of money. Adequate facilities are the very first step toward a basic computer literacy program. Many campuses are providing this widespread usage by expanding their base of microcomputers, as well as extending the terminal networks on larger computers. Throughout this book we will be examining effective ways of expanding the campus base.

Access means that students, faculty, administrators, and staff will have computing facilities in their *regular place of work or study*. Since the beginning of the computer era, *centralized facilities* have been the method of organizing computer services. A large computer and its associated paraphernalia were placed in a central location. Everyone had to adapt to the computer's schedules, work activities, and physical location needs. *The people adapted to the computer.* The next generation of "distributed" computing reverses the situation: *the computers will adapt to the people.* Instead of going to a central location people will have computers at their normal work place or study place—in their offices, in their homes, in their dorm rooms. Although in the short run this may not be possible, it should be the fundamental objective of every campus computing program. In Chapter 7 we expand on the access issue.

Let us look at one example of the "access" issue in a major university. Stanford University recently found that 25 percent of its staff and faculty members are "computing" at home (Margarrell, 1983). Within the next five years, this number is expected to climb to 60 percent. Staff and faculty members expect to do one-fifth of their work at home via a cable link to their offices. When asked how they would use their "university-linked home computers," the most common answers were text editing, sending information to a high-quality printer, accessing library material, managing and storing data, sending and receiving office communications, and utilizing Stanford Data Bases. Sixty percent of the faculty and staff members now use a computer of some kind at work. For those who do have home computers the time spent on the computer varies. Fifty percent use the computer one hour a day, 20 percent about two hours, and 4 percent are using their personal computers five hours or more.

Step Four: Develop Purchase Plans for Faculty and Students

The name of the game is access. People need more opportunities to use computing facilities actively. One way to maximize access is for the users to own their own computers. When computers had million-dollar price tags, ownership was utterly unthinkable for the individual. Now, however, the microcomputer has drastically lowered prices, and individual faculty, staff, and administrators can purchase microcomputers for their own departments and even for their own homes. Even students can afford microcomputers when the college or university carefully designs student purchase plans. A purchase program is an integral part of a campus-wide computing program.

For example, Rochester Institute of Technology has developed a plan that requires all its students to become computer literate by the time they graduate (Margarrell, 1983a). In order to encourage students, faculty, and staff members to buy their own computers, the institute has worked out an agreement with the Digital Equipment Corporation to offer discounts. For example, a $4,800 system is available for $2,800. Other ways in which Rochester Institute of Technology is making computers affordable are financing plans, leases with options to buy, two or more parties sharing any of these plans, and including the computer under the education category when student aid is calculated. The push to buy computers will not affect tuition rates and will be strictly voluntary. Laboratories with similar equipment will be available on campus for those who choose not to lease or buy. In Chapter 7 other purchase plans are discussed.

Step Five: Consider Networking Issues Carefully

In the old days (that is, two or three years ago) there was really no need to consider networking issues. Usually a campus had a large computer with a network of terminals. This provided total networking but probably resulted in low user accessibility. By contrast, a few campuses had clusters of stand-alone microcomputers, not linked to the larger computers or to each other. An either/or situation was common: large computers were networked to terminals; microcomputers were not linked at all. With new technological advances on the horizon, it will soon be possible to do sophisticated networking with groups of microcomputers. One model links the microcomputers among themselves to form a "local area network" that shares facilities such as printers and disk drives. The other model is to link the microcomputers up to larger computers so that they can exchange files and distribute work between the larger and the smaller computers. Any campus examining computer issues must look carefully at how much networking is appropriate, how much will it cost, and what the benefits will be. In Chapter 10 we will discuss networking in more detail.

Step Six: Plan and Implement Faculty and Staff Training Programs

A broad-based training program for faculty, staff, and administrators is essential. One of the terrific advantages of microcomputers, of course, is that they can be easily learned. Some campuses have used that ease of learning as an excuse: "We don't need a training effort because everybody can teach themselves." Well, this may be true to some extent, but self-learning is basically an *inefficient* way to manage the experience for an entire campus. Experience suggests that a college can speed up the learning process by mounting a coordinated, effective training program. The "learn it yourself" model can work, but it is inefficient, slow, and expensive. From the *institution's* point of view an effective training program has many advantages: (1) *faster* learning; (2) *broader* coverage; (3) *coordinated* learning that can bring along whole departments; (4) more *sophis-*

ticated levels of learning; (5) more *cost-effective* learning. Chapter 8 discusses training activities in more detail.

Step Seven: Promote Curriculum Change and Adaptation

One reason we stress the need for a full training program for faculty, as opposed to individual learning, is the need for curriculum innovation. When a whole *group* of faculty are learning together, a "snowballing" of expertise is likely to occur. Group learning triggers interest among faculty to experiment with curriculum changes.

There are many innovative ways in which computers can be used in the curriculum, far beyond the traditional research uses for graduate students and computer science for undergraduates. The possibilities now exist for fruitful, productive use of computers *throughout* the curriculum, spreading even into the previously non-computer-oriented liberal arts. The possibilities are endless: word processing in English composition, statistics in the social sciences, computer-assisted instruction in languages, math, and remedial education. All these, and many more, will be examined in Chapter 9.

THE COMPUTERIZATION OF CARNEGIE-MELLON

Carnegie-Mellon has made a reputation as an institution with big plans for the computerization of its campus. The following few pages are quoted, with permission, from an article by Charles S. Farrell in the *Chronicle of Higher Education* (1983). Note how the various steps we described above are being implemented at Carnegie-Mellon.

The Computer and Louis XVI

What Louis XVI needed was a computer.

In May, 1779, the French monarch knew there was trouble in his realm; so, with an eye toward reform, he encouraged the people to submit their particular grievances to the crown.

The response was overwhelming: Thousands of Frenchmen let the King know of their dissatisfactions. The outpouring more than underscored the need for reform, but the sheer volume of the grievances made evaluating them an awesome task. Louis, never a strong decision maker, remained in a quandary.

Within two months the Bastille was stormed and the French Revolution had begun.

Almost 200 years later, the "data" Louis XVI collected are being closely scrutinized and analyzed with the help of computers by history students at Carnegie-Mellon University here.

THE MODEST PLAN OF A SMALL COLLEGE: COLLEGE OF NOTRE DAME

Most of the press attention has focused on grand-scale campus computer projects such as Carnegie-Mellon's massive enterprise reported in this chapter. But small colleges, too, have been adapting themselves to the computer. The College of Notre Dame, a small liberal arts college in Belmont, California, is one example. Michael Donnellan, vice-president, describes his campus's activities:

Goal

There is a strong desire to enable all students, not just the majors, to achieve some computer competency if their ambitions and aspirations of a college education are to be realized. There is an equally strong commitment to explore the value-related dimensions of computers and education. The goal at the College of Notre Dame is to demonstrate how computers can be a resource for the liberal arts, as well as to determine how the liberal arts can explore the values of computer use.

A Story

Not unlike other four-year colleges of similar size and scope, the College of Notre Dame was caught off-guard by the "computer revolution." The response to this new technology was more haphazard than systematic. Inevitably, business administration and math departments took the biggest share of expenditure for hardware. This direction ignored a wider application of the computer across the curriculum. Likewise, little attention was given to the need for training to develop computer competency on a campus-wide basis for faculty, staff, and administration. In the meantime, admissions staff were continuing to report a shift of interest from prospective students away from liberal arts to computer science programs. In short, the story of the computer on campus was without much revolutionary fervor. For the noninvolved, the revolution seemed to result in some program areas being better funded than others, and that at the expense of liberal studies. The outlook was for more of the same.

A Plan

Impetus for a change of direction coincided with a heightened awareness about the function of computers on campus. With the help of a consultant a comprehensive plan began to unfold. This plan had five major, related components. First, there would be a *training program* open to all college personnel who wished to participate. Second, there would be a *single hardware system*. Both faculty and administration would receive training on the same system. Third, there would be commitment to develop software for *administrative application,* which would match the hardware capability. Fourth, there would be provision for the appointment of *key individuals* to coordinate the instructional lab and the management information system and to insure in-house expertise for further training. Fifth, there would be a *purchase plan* to enable faculty and students to purchase their own hardware. To sum up, this plan would encompass a total campus involvement and thereby be more truly "revolutionary" in its impact.

The computer enables them to sort through the thousands of grievances in a short period of time, allowing them to determine such things as the percentage of nobles, members of the bourgeoisie, clergymen, and peasants who shared certain dissatisfactions.

1,000 Work Stations

At Carnegie-Mellon, computers not only help students do historical research, they have invaded virtually every phase of the university's operations, creating a revolution in their own right.

About 75 per cent of Carnegie-Mellon's 5,500 students use the time-sharing computer system each day. There are about 1,000 computer work stations available on the campus, and most faculty members and administrators have terminals in their offices or at home.

Students and faculty members use the machines to send messages to each other, eliminating the need for much of the intracampus mail. Faculty members use the computer system to conduct research, and most students compose their term papers and other assignments on a computer screen.

Besides obvious applications in mathematics and other sciences, the computer is used to teach everything from the rudiments of writing to architecture; even spelling can be checked by computer. Artists can paint with an electronic palette with millions of color variations. Drama students can create scenery. A computer program is even being developed that will allow piano students to learn the proper spacing of notes.

The next step in Carnegie-Mellon's computer revolution will be to equip every student, faculty member, and staff member with his own personal computer.

Agreement with IBM

Last October, the university entered into a cooperative agreement with the International Business Machines Corporation to develop over the next three to five years a revolutionary academic computer system at an estimated cost of $20 million.

Douglas E. Van Houweling, vice-provost for computing and planning, says the arrangement between Carnegie-Mellon and IBM began after the university decided what it wanted in the summer of 1981.

"We didn't want to be the sole users of the system" he says, "so we wanted to do it in collaboration with a partner in major information processing."

Several other companies showed an interest in the project, Mr. Van Houweling says, but IBM went on to propose a joint study. Several of the company's computer experts arrived at Carnegie Mellon in November, 1981, he says, and after six months the experts and the university decided the project was "feasible and that IBM had the technology and corporate goals to work with us."

By the end of this decade, Carnegie-Mellon hopes to have a campus-wide network of 7,500 personal computers. Each will be able to operate independently, and will connect with every other personal computer on the campus and with the central computing and data-base facilities.

The agreement with IBM also calls for the creation of an information-technology center at Carnegie-Mellon, with staff members from both the company and the university. IBM will provide the money and equipment for the center and will retain marketing rights to all technology developed there.

Students will be required to pay an as-yet-undecided price each year for their personal computers. When they graduate, the computers will become their property.

Eventually, the system would enable students and alumni anywhere, at any time, to tie into Carnegie-Mellon's computer network and get, exchange, or provide information.

In announcing the agreement with IBM, Richard M. Cyert, president of Carnegie-Mellon, predicted that the personal computer would have "the same role in student learning that the development of the assembly line in the 1920's had for the production of automobiles."

"The assembly line enabled large-scale manufacturing to develop," he said. "Likewise, the network personal computer system will enable students to increase significantly the amount of learning they do in the university."

"Computer U"

The massive plan has led some critics of it to complain that Carnegie-Mellon will become "Computer U," churning out computer wizards who have mastered little else. It is a notion Carnegie-Mellon administrators are working hard to dispel.

"We want CMU to be a place where everybody uses computers, but not a place where everybody is a computing expert," Mr. Van Houweling says.

But why so computer-oriented? Because information processing has become such a fundamental part of society, and there is no faster way to process information than by computer.

"The notion is that the time of faculty members and students is valuable," Mr. Van Houweling says. "The computer can take time and make it more effective. Computers increase the ability to know more. You are better able to deal with a broad level of education."

While many other colleges and universities are bringing computers to their campuses and stressing computer literacy, Carnegie-Mellon is "creating a new environment for higher education," says Brian J. L. Berry, dean of the school of urban and public affairs.

"Others are not talking about transforming an environment," he says. "For better or for worse, this institution with its technology base, has decided to take the high-technology path and develop itself into a high-technological university."

Both Mr. Berry an Mr. Van Houweling acknowledge that there is concern about moral and ethical use of computers. Part of the money from IBM is being used to underwrite a study of the effects of computerization on the university and its students.

One question that has already been raised is whether students will use their computers to cheat—either by submitting on the computer material not their own or by stealing information from various sources.

The possibility of cheating has always existed, Mr. Berry says, and computers simply provide another way to do it.

"Whether or not we'll see an increase of abuse is dependent on what our beliefs are about standard behavior, and individual beliefs of what is right and wrong," he says. "This is a matter of ethics, and the computer is neutral. Unscrupulous people can use any device to be unscrupulous."

Mr. Van Houweling says he has heard the horror stories about students breaking computer codes and wreaking havoc. But in any setting there are penalties for wrongdoing, he says. "We have to develop the same set of norms for the computer. We have to try to understand a social norm for a computerized society. Constantly in our professional lives, we get information we're not really supposed to have."

While administrators and faculty members seem content to wait until the completion of the IBM financed study to determine what adverse effects computers may have, many students think the concerns need to be addressed now. Also, some students are bitter about what they see as a lack of student participation in the computer-planning process.

Bruce D. Werner, a senior majoring in mechanical engineering and public policy who helped design computerized aid for teaching fluid mechanics, says he supports the basics of the university's computerization plan, but he thinks students need to be more involved in the decisions.

"I'd like to see it succeed," he says, "but the administration has to think this out and treat the students as an integral part of the plan. Students can make the administrators' lives a pain."

"If the administrators want this to come off, they have to treat us right. We feel like we're cut off."

Mr. Werner says students learned of the IBM deal through newspaper accounts.

Anxiety Among Students

Christopher Johnston, a sophomore creative-writing major and assistant news editor of "The Tartan," the student newspaper, agrees that there has been a lack of student participation. He feels students are being ignored by the administration because by the time the computers start arriving *en masse* in 1986, most of today's students will be gone.

He adds that he and other students are also critical of the plan because the administration has stressed the good points but not the potential bad points.

"There is real anxiety among some students," Mr. Johnston says. "They're afraid. It is as if the technology is overrunning us and stealing our ididuality."

Mr. Johnston says students are also concerned about protecting computers from being stolen from their dormitory rooms, about getting behind in their studies should their computers break, and about the possible psychological effects of sitting at a computer terminal for long periods of time.

If there are answers to those questions, they haven't been given to students, he says.

Nathan Solano, president of the student government, says many students are questioning the cost of personal computers, which to some will be nothing more than a glorified typewriter.

He also questions the importance the university has placed on computerization at a time when there is a shortage of classroom space. He says some students have taken to referring sarcastically to the information technology center, now under construction, as "the student union" because, despite pleas from students, the campus has no student union.

John P. Crecine, dean of the college of humanities and social services, says there is "probably some truth" in the accusation that students aren't involved in the planning process. But he says, after initial agreement among administrators, faculty members, and students that equipping everyone with personal computers was the next step, it was decided that the details of doing so should be left to experts.

Developing "Courseware"

Self-confessed "computer nut" Alex Czajkowski, a senior majoring in technical-and-professional writing, disagrees with students who complain that they haven't been involved in planning Carnegie-Mellon's entrance into the world of computers. "Students *are* getting involved—but they have to take the initiative."

Students are not only helping to plan the massive computer network, Mr. Czajkowski says, but are also helping to develop programs, or "courseware," that can be used in teaching and research.

When more computer programs are developed to help students learn, Carnegie-Mellon officials believe, teachers will be able to devote more of their time to improving their teaching.

David Kaufer, an assistant professor of English who helped develop the university's computerized writing program, says computers are worth the money they cost because "they free teachers to teach the things they can best teach."

Without computers, teachers of writing and other subjects spend a great deal of time going over the rudiments. The endless repetition bores the teacher, Mr. Kaufer says, making him or her less effective.

The computer takes care of the basics, he says, and is available to the student at times when a teacher is not. That, according to Mr. Kaufer, "allows the teachers to be real specialists in teaching writing and teaching the importance of judgement and good reasoning."

Mr. Kaufer sees the computer as an invaluable educational tool. "In the next decade," he says, "for a kid to grow up without a computer will be like being without a calculator or a TV set today. The consequences of not having a computer in that society will be too great."

Dependence on Computers?

Will people become dependent on computers, much as many people today need a calculator to perform even the simplest mathematical tasks?

Mr. Van Houweling says that not to use computers would be like not using the telephone, which people have grown accustomed to and dependent on—as they will to computers. Like the telephone, the computer is designed to help people do things more easily, he says.

He adds that because of its speed the computer should allow students to complete their work in less time, giving them the freedom to do other things.

Could the computerization of Carnegie-Mellon turn off potential students who might otherwise be interested in attending the university?

That possibility exists, Mr. Van Houweling admits. Potential applicants will have to understand that Carnegie-Mellon "is dedicated to providing them with a tool to do a better job," he says. "I hope the quality of applicants goes up, but that the composition, in other respects, doesn't change."

Hopes That Others Will Follow

Mr. Van Houweling stresses that the additional cost to students of the computers will be taken into account in calculating financial aid.

Carnegie-Mellon considers itself a leader in using computers in education, and hopes that other institutions will follow it, Mr. Van Houweling says.

"Personally, I would not be upset because everybody caught up with us," he says. "I think it would be great for higher education if we get to the point where every working professor has a computer and the knowledge of what to do with it. It would be most productive if Congress earmarked money to provide universities with the equipment to be as productive as we plan to be."

Or, as Marie Antoinette might have put it, "Let them use FORTRAN."

CHAPTER 3

MICROCOMPUTERS: THE MACHINES

AND THEIR ROLE ON CAMPUS

Like people, computers come in all shapes and sizes. They do many different tasks.

TYPES OF COMPUTERS

Most of the computer profession crudely divides computers into three types: mainframes, minicomputers, and microcomputers. Let us briefly examine each type.

Mainframe Computers

Mainframe computers, extremely large machines with phenomenal computing capacities, are the giants of the computer world. These are the computers that NASA uses to send a man to the moon, that the energy department uses to build an atom bomb, that the University of California uses to run its administrative data systems, that the American Telephone and Telegraph Company uses for a worldwide communication system. Mainframe computers can have hundreds of users simultaneously. In addition, they can perform dozens of different tasks for those users. Mainframe computers cost millions of dollars, require large staffs of people to operate them, require constant service, and demand special real estate to house them.

Minicomputers

These middle-sized computers are smaller than the mainframes and consequently are called "minicomputers." The distinction between mainframes and minicomputers is not sharp; only a rough sense of size separates them. Some minicomputer manufacturers want to sound grandiose and will call their minicomputer a mainframe. But when all is said and done, the rule of thumb is that minicomputers are the middle-sized

26

machines. They have the capability to run up to one hundred users at a single time, will perform multiple tasks, and probably cost no more than $1 million. At the low end, some minicomputers cost less than $100,000. Minicomputers are often used for specialized tasks: a chemistry department in a college, a registrar's operation in a university, an inventory control system for a grocery chain, or an accounting operation in a factory.

Microcomputers

The smallest machines are the desktop microcomputers. The Apple Computer Company almost singlehandedly revolutionized the computing world by popularizing the small microcomputer for home, school, and office. Originally the microcomputer was a toy for hobbyists, built in a garage by kids with green eyeshades who played exciting computer games. Microcomputers gradually became more sophisticated. The giants of the computer world, even IBM, now turn to the microcomputer as the wave of the future.

Differentiating microcomputers from mainframes and minis is relatively simple the micro sits on your desk and the others require huge installations. But basically they all do the same thing. Again, the differentiation is crudely a matter of capacity and cost, with microcomputers at the lower end. Nowadays you can purchase a barely functional microcomputer for less than a hundred dollars, and for $4,000 you can acquire a truly effective system.

In short, the computer world can be crudely divided into mainframes, minicomputers, and microcomputers. Examine Table 3-1 to see some distinguishing features.

THE COMPONENTS OF A MICROCOMPUTER

Although a detailed knowledge of computer technology is not required to use a computer, some overall understanding will help guide administrative decision making in selecting and using a computer system. It is probably more feasible for an administrator to gain a functional knowledge of a computer system's operation than for the computer specialist to fully comprehend the administrator's complex needs and concerns. This section gives a brief overview of the computer hardware and software.

A microcomputer, also known as a personal computer (PC) or a desktop computer, is an electronic device with several components, working for a single user. Microcomputers have the same components as major computers, but on a much smaller scale. A typical microcomputer system will have 48,000 to 256,000 characters of internal memory, a keyboard, a monitor (TV screen), one or two floppy diskette drives, and a printer.

TABLE 3-1. COMPARING THREE TYPES OF COMPUTERS

	Mainframe Computers	Minicomputers	Microcomputers
1. Users	Large number (50+)	Medium (10–60)	One
2. Programs	Several simultaneously	Several simultaneously	Usually only one at a time
3. Cost	Extremely expensive, ($350,000–$1 million or more)	Expensive ($50,000–$300,000)	Low cost ($3,000–$10,000)
4. Installation	Complex, long-term process	Complex, long-term process	Single, immediate process
5. Technical Repair Support	On-site centralized, and expensive	Service contract; on-site staff	Take into repair center
6. Staff Support	Large, full-time staff	Some full-time staff	No central staff required
7. Programming	Complex, customized, expensive	Complex, customized; expensive	Simple, software plus options for custom programs; inexpensive
8. User Access	Requires intensive training and data management expertise	Requires intensive training and data management expertise	Easy and immediate; not dependent upon extensive training
9. Critical Problems	Cost; dependence on expertise; centralization; user training; developing software	Cost; dependence on expertise; centralization; user training; developing software	Limited computer capacity; evolving technology; highly technical tasks not always possible
10. Major Benefits	Enormous computing power and capacity; supports large number of users; very complex and specialized tasks	Lower cost than main-frames; computing power for large tasks; multiple users	Decentralized; user-friendly software for immediate applications; interactive links to minis and mainframe; inexpensive hardware and software

Microcomputers are currently available from several manufacturers, and all have similar characteristics. In late 1983 the most commonly known desktop computers, listed in alphabetical order by manufacturer, were:

Apple II, IIe, III, Lisa
Commodore PET and Model 64
DEC Rainbow 100, Decmate II, Professional 300 series
IBM Personal Computer, IBM XT
Osborne Portable
Radio Shack TRS-80 I, II, and III

No list of desktop computers can remain current for long, so this list does not purport to be inclusive. Currently there are over 150 brands of microcomputers.

Desktop computers are composed of several components, which may be built into a single unit, or may be separate units cabled together. Figure 3-1 shows a configuration for a typical microcomputer, and each major component is described in the following pages.

FIGURE 3-1. MICROCOMPUTER COMPONENT ILLUSTRATION

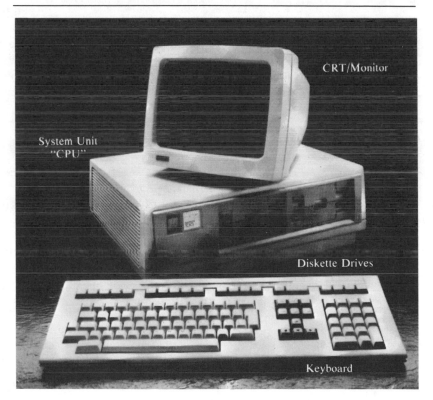

Central Processing Unit

The central processing unit (CPU) is the central device of any desktop computer: the "brain" that directs all the computer's activities. This unit is divided into three main parts: the arithmetic/logic unit (ALU), the primary storage unit, and the control unit.

The Arithmetic/Logic Unit (ALU). The ALU is responsible for actually processing or manipulating the data by performing arithmetic computations or logical operations such as adding, subtracting, or comparing two numbers. The ALU can be thought of as the absent-minded genius who can calculate at the speed of light but cannot remember the answer or who asked the question. Thus, the computer also needs storage units to help it remember things.

Storage Units: RAM and ROM. The primary storage unit, also known as Random-Access Memory (RAM), stores all input. The contents in primary storage are "volatile," that is, when the computer is turned off the contents are lost. The computer also has permanent, nonvolatile memory called Read-Only Memory (ROM). ROM memory never goes away and is used for storing operating procedures for the machine itself. Thus RAM is temporary information you are working with currently; ROM is a set of information that constantly remains in the machine to make it operate smoothly.

Storage sizes are described in "K" bytes where each "K" is equal to 1,024 units. Thus a computer with 256K bytes of memory can store $256 \times 1,024 = 262,144$ characters. Most desktop computers come with a base memory size, and additional modules of memory can be added. Currently, 256K is about the largest standard memory, although machines with as much as 1000K (a "megabyte") have recently emerged (e.g., DEC Micro-PDP 11 and Apple Lisa).

Often a computer is described as being an eight-bit computer or a sixteen-bit computer. This refers to the "word size" or the number of bits that can be manipulated by the computer at one time. The longer the word length, the more data the computer can handle. Simply stated, the longer the word length, the more sophisticated and powerful the computer.

The Control Unit. The control unit is responsible for directing and controlling the activities of the computer. Its circuitry works in conjunction with the "operating system," which will be discussed later. The control unit is the traffic cop insuring a smooth flow of traffic. This unit does not store or manipulate data, rather it "communicates" with the outside world by accepting input, putting it into storage, and channeling output to the outside world.

The Whole Process: An Analogy

This entire process is analogous to many everyday situations. Take the example of dining at a restaurant. You sit down and read the menu. Then the waiter (control unit) takes your order (input) and puts the ticket on the order wheel (primary storage) where it remains until the cook (ALU) reads it and prepares the meal according to your request (input data). The cook reads the recipe (instructions) and sets the meal (results) on the counter (primary storage) where it waits for the waiter (control unit) to take it back to the table (output) so that you (user) can enjoy your favorite meal.

Other Major Components

In addition to the central processing unit described above, there are many other important components.

Monitors. A monitor is basically a TV screen. With appropriate connectors a standard black and white or color TV set may be used as a monitor. However, the image is less clear than with a monitor designed for use with computers. Most desktop computer manufacturers offer their own monitor; however, many are interchangeable. Also, some monochromatic monitors are black and white, while others are amber or green. Color monitors with high resolution are quite expensive ($800 and up) but are very effective with graphics.

Disk Drives. Disk drives read and write data on a floppy diskette for off-line storage. Many desktop computers have space designed for one or more diskette drives in the system unit, and additional drives may be attached. Most desktop computers operate with disk drives that use five $\frac{1}{4}$ inch diskettes that can store between 150,000 and 500,000 characters each. Some desktop computers operate with 3-inch disks, and others have 8-inch diskette drives. As with system unit memory, diskette character capacities are usually referred to in K units of 1,024, for example 128K. *Hard disks* that will store millions of characters are also available. For reference, one million characters is referred to as one megabyte.

Keyboards. Keyboards for desktop computers are similar to the standard typewriter keyboard, except that they usually have additional keys for specific functions. Many microcomputer keyboards also contain a numeric keypad for easy entry of numbers. Some keyboards are integrated with the system unit and others are attached by cable for flexible operation. The new PCjr from IBM uses a novel keyboard that is not attached with wires, but instead uses an infrared signal from keyboard to computer. Sometimes, as additional features are needed, keyboard "templates" are supplied by either the computer manufacturer or by a software company to redefine some keys for specific functions.

Printers. Printers for desktop computers are usually small, eighty characters per second (cps) dot matrix printers that can print on continuous paper. Less expensive printers print on thermal paper. More expensive "daisy wheel" impact printers may be attached for letter quality output. Since the printer is the key link between information and the end user, the choice of a proper printer is an important decision.

Other Equipment. Other devices such as plotters, graphic input tablets,

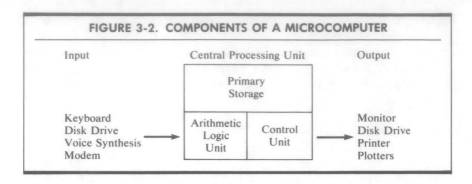

FIGURE 3-2. COMPONENTS OF A MICROCOMPUTER

test scoring machines, bar-code readers, electronic typewriters, and game "joy-sticks" may also be attached to microcomputers. The communication equipment, called a "modem," that will connect your computer to the telephone for conversation with other computers may also be added. Figure 3-2 lists the major microcomputer components and how they relate to one another.

THE DEBATE OVER MICROCOMPUTERS

Microcomputers have gained widespread acceptance in the home and in business. But college campuses, where computing has been common for decades, have sometimes been slow in introducing microcomputers. The computer priesthood, the computer science specialists, and the computer center directors have not always moved quickly to pick up on the microcomputer revolution.

The Critics' Complaints

Critics have in the past raised several complaints against microcomputers:

- ○ Microcomputers do not have enough power—we already have a mainframe and we don't need a proliferation of microcomputers.
- ○ The software for microcomputers does not have the power of larger systems.
- ○ We already have large sunk costs in our large computers. It is inefficient to introduce microcomputers on top of that sunk cost.
- ○ Microcomputers can never furnish specialized services such as large number-crunching and exotic graphics.

Most objections levied by critics of microcomputers are *technical*. The arguments about capacity, specialized uses, and raw power are constantly marshaled to explain why big computers are more effective than microcomputers.

There is a fundamental flaw in these objections. It is true that the million-dollar computers will have more capacity than small microcomputers. And of course, for extremely specialized tasks, such as handling large data bases, microcomputers lose their competitive edge. But for most people microcomputers will be sufficient for most tasks. The question is not whether a $5,000 machine can accomplish the same task as a $1 million machine. *The real issue is the ratio between cost and effectiveness.* We believe that for many situations microcomputers are dramatically more cost effective than massive mainframes and minicomputers.

In short, it is not the question of which machine is *better*, but which machine is better for *which task, which user, and at what cost?* Cost effectiveness, not raw power, is the issue. Big computers will always win the raw power test. But on the cost effective test, the little computers are often the best option for the money spent.

Many Objections Are Based on Organizational Power Questions

Technical questions of raw capacity and sunk costs are prevalent at meetings. But we have a gut suspicion that many objections to microcomputers are based on organizational politics. The priesthood has an empire to protect. Introducing microcomputers could be a big threat to that empire, for people might not come to the temple to worship. Instead they might work with their own microcomputers wherever they needed them. If microcomputers allow users to control their own fate, the budgets for the computer center might not grow as fast and the new computing personnel might not be as readily obtainable. In short, the power base of some people might be eroded when people acquire microcomputers and simply start using them any way they please!

The critics object on technical and political grounds, but the microcomputer advocates respond on *user need* grounds. The critics charge, "Bigger computers have more power; the computer center can provide the service through terminals if we have enough money." The microcomputer advocates respond: "We're willing to sacrifice raw power if we can control our own computing. User control and user-friendly software are the real issues for us."

Fortunately, most enlightened priesthood members have changed their tune. Usually the priesthood's conversion to microcomputers is honest; they come to believe that decentralized microcomputing is the future trend. In a few cases their conversion may be a political necessity—the microcomputer wave is going to wash over them anyway, so they decide to swim with the flow. In either case, most people in the priesthood are now actively advocating microcomputers. In the next few months and years most computer users will embrace microcomputing wholeheartedly.

Incidentally, one reason the priesthood usually embraces microcomputers now is the widespread experience that adding micros actually promotes the use of mainframes and minicomputers. Many campuses find that as people get hooked on computing through the use of micros they turn to larger computers for more sophisticated applications. In short, rather than micros stealing part of a fixed computing pie, the new-found enthusiasm prompted by micros helps enlarge the pie.

The Debate over Microcomputers Is Diminishing

The College and University Systems Exchange (CAUSE) is a professional association for the development, use, and management of information systems in American higher education. CAUSE has been conducting training seminars to acquaint computer center directors and other administrators with the applications, versatility, and power of microcomputers. It is particularly revealing to find CAUSE, the professional association whose members have traditionally been the champions of expensive mainframe computers, arguing for the microcomputer as part of campus computing networks.

At a 1983 workshop in Boulder, Colorado, Charles Thomas, executive director of CAUSE, was asked about common objections to microcomputers. His response, recorded by one of our authors and used with his permission, was instructive:

> Most objections to microcomputers are, quite frankly, based on lack of knowledge. The field has changed so dramatically that most people simply just don't realize and just won't believe that you can get a serious, powerful computer on your desk. Coupled with a hard-disk drive, these machines have tremendous storage capacity. Moreover, you can link microcomputers into networks with larger machines. And the advantages are fantastic—low-cost, user-friendly software, and enormous versatility. The issue is not microcomputers *versus* other computers. Rather, the issue is flexible, useful computer systems. The objective is to build and maintain rich computing options, to train people to *really use these machines,* and to keep multiple avenues open. Both the large computers and the microcomputers have a role in multifaceted, flexible systems.
>
> Of course there are functions where microcomputers would be inappropriate—large number-crunching, student registration—anything that requires thousands of data entries. But there are many activities which do not require a large computer, and which are ideal for microcomputers. For example, why tie up main computer capacity for doing word processing that is more conveniently done on a micro? Why teach administrators the complexities of financial analyses on a mainframe when a Visicalc software makes it easy on a micro? Why purchase costly mainframe graphics programs when low-cost microcomputer software can usually do an adequate job for a small fraction of the cost?
>
> In short, we need both options; institutions will need a mixture of various computers.

SOME ADVANTAGES OF MICROCOMPUTERS

Let us quickly run through the Big Ten, namely, the ten major advantages of microcomputers. (To be fair, we will later mention some disadvantages of microcomputers).

1. Microcomputers Have an Excellent Ratio Between Cost and Usefulness

Microcomputers will not do everything that a million-dollar mainframe will do. But for the money spent, the cost-effectiveness ratio is excellent. For reasonable small costs you can do an enormous amount of work.

2. Microcomputers Can Be Quickly Installed and People Can Be Quickly Trained to Use Them

One big disappointment with large computers is the enormous lag between the decision to buy one and its real use in your everyday situation. By contrast, microcomputers can be installed almost instantaneously, and the training period for staff is a fraction of that required for large computers. Charles Thomas calls it "shortening the time interval to real productivity."

3. Microcomputers Increase the Flexibility of Existing Campus Networks

On almost any campus microcomputers will increase the variety and flexibility of computing. More people will use computers; they will use different programs; and they will apply them to a broader spectrum of problems. Certainly this increased flexibility is an important advantage.

4. Microcomputer Software is Cheap and Readily Available

Microcomputers will not do everything, and their software is rarely as sophisticated as that for larger computers. Nevertheless, microcomputer software is perfectly adequate for many tasks. For tasks that can be handled by microcomputers the software is ridiculously cheap compared to larger computer software. We have entered an era of "disposable software" where the users can experiment with many cheap software packages to find the best for their needs.

5. A Decentralized Microcomputer Network Does Not Go Down When One Unit Fails

The experience is miserable. Right in the middle of our computer job the "system goes down." And when that nerve center collapses all the users go down with it! By contrast, on a campus with decentralized microcomputers the failure of one unit will not crash the whole system. A user with a critical job who has a failure can simply move to another machine and keep working. "System crash," that familiar demon of the big computer, is a rare problem with a network of microcomputers.

6. Microcomputers Maximize Local Control and Decentralization

A centralized big machine encourages centralization: centralized decisions about what software to buy, centralized control over usage, centralized decisions about dollar charges, centralized choices about services to offer, centralized priority-setting for different people's work. But the story is dramatically different with the network of microcomputers. Now the user controls the machine, makes the decisions about what gets done, and decides what software to use. With mainframes the central priesthood is king; with microcomputers, the users are their own bosses!

7. Productivity Increases When Microcomputers Are Used

Two productivity questions could be asked here. First, does the use of microcomputers increase productivity compared to having no computers at all? For almost any task where a computer would be seriously considered the answer is an unambiguous yes. Compared to typing, a word processor is infinitely more sophisticated; compared to a paper spreadsheet, an electronic program does miracles for budgeting; compared to paper files, a data base management system is light-years ahead.

The second question is a little more tricky: do microcomputers increase productivity more than terminals linked up to a mainframe? That depends almost entirely on the task. For a task that requires a huge data base and specialized software a mainframe will increase productivity more than a micro. But for many other tasks, such as word processing and many curriculum applications, a microcomputer is better for productivity. One major advantage is that the microcomputer is simple enough for people to actually *use,* and the leap from no computer to any computer is the major productivity jump.

8. The Spread of Microcomputers May Slow the Increase in Computer Specialists

When more and more people become computer "generalists" we will have less need for more computer "specialists." We need to be careful here. We are not saying that the number of computer specialists will be reduced, only that the *ratio* of computer specialists to tasks accomplished will be reduced. In other words, you are going to get more things done with less input from the computer specialists. When everyone becomes a computer specialist, you will need fewer computer specialists on the payroll! Actually this is rather tricky logic, because we really expect the *absolute numbers* of computer specialists to increase, but the ratio of specialists to completed computer tasks will decrease. The main point here is that people will do their own computing, thus increasing the amount of actual work done.

TABLE 3-2. ADVANTAGES OF MICROCOMPUTERS
1. Low cost, high power
2. Quickly installed
3. Increases flexibility of system
4. Software—cheap and available
5. Avoids down time
6. Decentralized: local control is maximized
7. Productivity increases
8. Fewer IR and computer personnel
9. Very good security
10. Overall advantage: "user friendly"

9. Microcomputers Give Excellent Security for Sensitive Topics

How is security handled on a mainframe computer when sensitive topics are stored? Secret keys keep out unauthorized prying eyes. But the newspapers are full of stories about clever people who break these secret codes and steal millions of dollars from computers! With a microcomputer the secret of good security is ridiculously simple. You take the floppy disk containing sensitive information and lock it away. Barring a stick of dynamite, your floppy disk and its secret information are protected.

10. Microcomputers Are "User-Friendly"

All these advantages combine into advantage Number Ten: the microcomputer is "user-friendly." That phrase is getting a little shopworn by now; it is used so much it is almost trite. But shopworn expressions usually have a grain of truth and this one is no exception. Microcomputers really *are* user-friendly, and that is one fundamental secret to their success. They work like serious computers and they function so the user can control them. Because microcomputers are so cheap and easy to use, and it is so easy to train people to operate them, they have substantial advantages over big "unfriendly" computers. Table 3-2 summarizes these advantages.

SOME DISADVANTAGES OF MICROS AND THE NEED FOR NETWORKS

In spite of all their advantages, microcomputers are not likely to replace mainframe and minicomputers in the near future. Although they handle many tasks well, microcomputers simply will not do everything. For the foreseeable future campuses will need to maintain large computers for specialized functions:

1. for applications that require huge number-crunching activities (example: massive mathematical and scientific problems)
2. for extremely sophisticated graphics functions (example: assisted engineering design work with "CADCAM")
3. for large data bases where many users must access the exact same files (examples: registration and registrar data)
4. for applications where all system users need instantaneous update on changes in data (example: student data files).

Certainly a microcomputer cannot yet operate a space shuttle, or manage a large university's student registration system, or provide sociologists with the tools for national opinion surveys, or give astronomers the calculating power they need. For these powerful, specialized applications we still need huge computers. But for a world of other mundane, down-to-earth applications microcomputers will do very well.

This is not an either/or situation. Most campuses will find they need large, medium, and small computers. The real issue is to develop a rich network of computing capabilities, with big computers to do big tasks and little computers to do little tasks. The basic goal is to create a flexible, multifaceted computing network.

Campuses will have many different kinds of computers. Now the critical question is how much *networking* should link all these machines? Some people argue that all micros must be hooked up to the mainframe, the Master Networking Plan. This is probably overkill and is more networking than the average campus can possibly use. And worse, it is back to the old centralized "octopus" theory of computing.

On most campuses it will not be necessary to hook everything up with everything else. Many microcomputers will perform their functions quite adequately without being connected in a network. Nevertheless, some networking is appropriate and will enhance the system's overall flexibility. Chapter 8 discusses this networking issue further.

THREE GENERATIONS OF MICROCOMPUTERS

Microcomputers have been around only a few years. The Apple Computer Company popularized the microcomputer, marketing its first Apple II machines in 1977. There were a few primitive microcomputers before that time but most people date the modern microcomputer trend from the Apple II's introduction. Since then scores of microcomputer brands have emerged and dozens of innovations have occurred in microcomputer technology.

A technical specialist might identify many stages in the development of microcomputers. Most popular writing identifies only two microcom-

TABLE 3-3. THREE GENERATIONS OF MICROCOMPUTERS

Characteristics	First	Second	Third
Processor	8 bit	8 bit	8/16 bit
Keyboard	poor	good	excellent
Memory (K-size)	16/48/64	64/128/256	64/1000K
Disk storage	160K	160–400	very large floppy and hard disks
Word processing	poor	good	excellent
Users	hobbyists programmers	managers professionals	managers professionals
Examples	Apple II TRS-80-III Atari Osborne I	Apple III Apple IIe TRS-80-II HP-125	DEC Rainbow Apple Lisa IBM-PC TI-PC HP-150

puter "generations," but for the academic administrator we think a useful division is three "generations."

First-Generation Microcomputers

Table 3-3 identifies the three basic microcomputer generations. The Apple II was the leading first-generation microcomputer. It had an eight-bit processing unit. That is, it could handle eight pieces of information simultaneously (a technical concept that we need not explore further). The Apple II opened the market for the home hobbyists, the people who would sit and program their own software and use it for small-scale functions. This was not a machine designed for heavy use. It had a rather clumsy keyboard, a screen that was only forty columns wide (standard manuscript paper is eighty columns wide), and small internal memory. In short, it was a very limited machine and was not practical for common office functions or for most scientific functions. Nevertheless, it was an inexpensive computer that actually worked, and the idea caught on like wildfire. Apple paved the way but other computers soon sprang up to take advantage of a rapidly growing market. The Radio Shack TRS-80 series was one of the biggest sellers alongside Apple. Many first-generation machines are still being made today, including most of the inexpensive models by Atari, Commodore, Timex, Radio Shack, Sinclair, and Osborne.

Second-Generation Microcomputers

Many computer specialists argue that the second generation began when sixteen-bit processing units arrived, but from a *user's* perspective the second generation began when the hobbyist's machine was transformed into an office workhorse. What the office and administrative user needed was a heavy-volume machine with more memory, a better keyboard, and an eighty-column screen. Professional, office, and administrative users wanted good word processing almost as their first requirement. The first-generation machines were poor word processors, with their forty-column screens and their primitive keyboards. So most microcomputer manufacturers realized that changes were needed to break into the professional and office market.

Consequently the leading manufacturers such as Apple and Radio Shack upgraded their original hobbyist machines into true professional and office products. The Apple III is a good example of the transformation. It has an elaborate keyboard with a numerical ten-key pad, up to 256K memory, and a standard eighty-column screen. Here was a machine designed for professional, administrative, and office use. Radio Shack followed suit with its TRS-80 Model II. Later, Apple issued an upgraded version of its old Apple II, called the Apple IIe. With its improved keyboard, upgraded memory, and eighty-column screen it qualifies as a second-generation machine in our taxonomy. Several other common microcomputers currently on the market fit into the second-generation category: the Franklin, the Hewlett-Packard 125, and the Osborne Executive.

Third-Generation Microcomputers

The IBM company finally decided that personal computers were here to stay, and in 1981 Big Blue entered the market with an advanced sixteen-bit central processing unit in its Personal Computer. A sixteen-bit chip handles sixteen information pieces at once, is more sophisticated than an eight-bit processor, and can use more sophisticated software. Most popular writers suggest that eight-bit machines were all in one generation and sixteen-bit machines are the second generation. We mentioned, however, some important distinctions, from the *user's* point of view, within the eight-bit group.

From the user's perspective there are two important advantages to a sixteen-bit processor: faster processing speed and the ability to use "multi-task" software. The eight-bit machines could do only one task at a time, for example, word processing. Most sixteen-bit software is also limited to one task, but multi-tasks are possible and some software manufacturers are seizing on that capability. The arrival of the IBM PC with its sixteen-bit processor exploded the microcomputer market. Where Apple and Radio Shack had a complete stranglehold over the eight-bit market, IBM took a commanding lead in the third-generation machines.

To summarize, then, third-generation machines have these characteristics:

1. sixteen-bit processor
2. an advanced keyboard with many special function keys
3. eighty-column screen
4. very powerful internal memories (up to a megabyte)
5. larger storage space, often including a hard disk drive as well as floppy disks (earlier machines could also use hard disks but rarely did).

In short, the third-generation machines were substantially more sophisticated than either the first or second generations.

IBM quickly achieved a towering lead in the third generation market. But many other manufacturers rushed in to fill a growing user base. The Digital Equipment Company (DEC) jumped into the market with a whole series of extremely sophisticated microcomputers, including the Rainbow 100, Decmate II, and Professional 300 series machines. In addition, dozens of IBM look-alikes were quickly spawned, trying to capitalize upon IBM's clear dominance in the third-generation machines.

FUTURE TRENDS AND DEVELOPMENTS

The technology of computers is exploding. Anything we say about the technology today will have to be revised tomorrow. The microcomputer began only in 1977, but the technological strides have been amazing. What will the future bring? We can only guess, of course, but here are a few predictions about the machines, the software, and their uses on college campuses.

Machines Will Continue to Decline in Cost

We mentioned earlier that computing power has been declining in cost at about 25 percent per year. That trend will be difficult to continue indefinitely—computers would soon be almost free! The cost of the machines will not drop to close to zero, as you might naturally assume if you continue to reduce prices by 25 percent! Nevertheless, the power and usefulness will continue to increase and the prices will decline modestly. To say it another way, the cost-benefit ratio will get better.

In late 1983 a number of dramatic price drops occurred. Item: at a Chicago technology marketing show, the Adam computer was introduced, which provided substantial computing power and many features for under a thousand dollars. The announcement shocked many competitors at that same trade show, although later there were major delivery problems with the machine. *Item:* during the summer the Apple Company discontinued the 128K version of its Apple III and dramatically dropped the price on the 256K version. *Item:* during the summer we received four different versions of the DEC microcomputer price list—and every version showed price drops over the last! *Item:* as this book is going to press the IBM "Peanut" machine has just been announced and it will constitute another major price break. *Item:* several companies announced last summer that their hard disk drives will be doubled from five to ten megabytes with no additional charge, an example of that increasing cost-benefit ratio.

Undoubtedly future machines will be cheaper per unit of computing power. Either the cost will go down or the capabilities will go up—both will most likely occur. Does this mean that campuses ought to wait until prices go down even further? If you have followed this book you know our answer: the real cost is in *human obsolescence.* It does not pay to wait for machine developments before you get your human potential moving. Remember, machine prices will be coming down but the cost of people services and training will be going up!

Memory Capacity and Storage Capacity Will Increase Dramatically

The internal memory (RAM) increases on each new generation of machines. The IBM PC can now be configured to over 700K; the Rainbow 100+ can upgrade to over 900K; the new Lisa from Apple has a megabyte (1,000K) of internal memory; and the new Micro PDP-11 from Digital can have an astonishing capacity of four megabytes of internal memory. And the price of this memory is declining rapidly. Your desktop computer in the future will have all the internal memory that the average user can possibly handle.

Mass storage is also increasing dramatically. One previous frustration of working with microcomputers was that large data bases simply would not fit on low-capacity floppy disks. Most floppy disks through 1981 had capacities of roughly 160K (about seventy typed pages), not a very impressive storage cabinet for a user with a large data base. Consequently, limitations on mass storage meant that microcomputers were not useful in many important managerial and educational settings.

The storage problem, however, is improving rapidly. On the one hand, the capacity of floppy disks is going up sharply. Several companies are now using double-sided, double-density disks, while others have developed quad-density disks. With those technologies, floppy disks can hold 400K to 500K of information. On the other hand, hard disk drives that will hold five or ten megabytes (5,000K or 10,000K) are becoming common for top-quality microcomputers. DEC, IBM, and Apple have all introduced hard disks into their microcomputer lines. With ten-megabyte hard disks and an internal RAM of 500K to a megabyte, we are now talking about serious, heavy-duty computing. There is every reason to assume that even greater mass storage will be included in the future generation of microcomputers.

Multiple User Micros Will Blur the Distinction with Minicomputers

Until recently the number of users was a clear distinguishing feature between a minicomputer and microcomputer. Minicomputers were multiple-user machines, while microcomputers were strictly single-user equipment. Desktop computers will soon allow multiple users, and the distinction between microcomputers and minicomputers will be totally blurred. Already the distinctions based on memory size, storage capacity, and software capability have diminished. Now the arrival of multi-user microcomputers will make it increasingly difficult to separate micros from minis. To the user they will all look the same; consequently, we will need to read the label on the machine and call it whatever the manufacturer names it!

The arrival of multi-user microcomputers is an ironic development. Much of the original rationale for microcomputers was the total independence they gave from larger computers. Does the trend toward multi-user microcomputers suggest that computing will be recentralized just as we were winning the war for decentralization?

The multi-user microcomputer is already available for purchase, offered by several smaller, less well-known companies. In addition, the Digital Equipment Company (DEC) is now marketing a Micro PDP-11 and a Micro Vax, both multi-user microcomputers based on the popular DEC minicomputer series. The machines have been so popular that the manufacturing arm of DEC cannot fill the orders for these machines. At a price of approximately $20,000 (in the summer of 1983) the fully configured machine with five or six users is very cost-effective. The future will see many more developments along this line, and the distinction between minicomputers and microcomputers may almost vanish. Table 3-4 lists the future trends in microcomputers.

TABLE 3-4. FUTURE TRENDS IN DESKTOP COMPUTING EQUIPMENT

1. Smaller, faster machines
2. Increased cost effectiveness
3. Larger memory
4. Hard disks, greater storage
5. Improved displays, graphics
6. Improved printers
7. Advanced networking

CHAPTER 4

THE SOFTWARE

REVOLUTION

The arrival of inexpensive, powerful microcomputers is only half the story. The other half of the equation is the dramatic change in software, the programs that actually drive the computer and do the work. Without adequate software the microcomputer is a fancy typewriter keyboard with nothing to do. Although attention focuses on the machine, in reality much attention ought to focus on the software. There are two basic kinds of software: systems software and applications software. Systems software makes the hardware work; they help the computer run quickly and efficiently. Applications software contains instructions written by a programmer that tell the computer to perform a certain task desired by the user. Rapid expansion of the microcomputer market has given rise to many software companies that write and distribute application programs for almost any use you can imagine. Specialized uses still exist, however, and these require the trained skills of a programmer. Fortunately, the increasing sophistication of programming languages has made this task easier over the years.

SYSTEMS SOFTWARE

There are several types of systems software, the programs that actually drive the machine. *Processing programs* are used to simplify program preparation and execution. Some of the main processing programs are the compilers, assemblers, and interpreters (language translator programs). These language translator programs convert the programming language being used by the programmer (source code) into machine language (object code) that the machine can understand.

The most important part of the systems software is the *operating system*. The operating system is the interface between the hardware and the applications software the user wants to operate. The software that runs on one operating system is not compatible or cannot run on a different operating system.

Consequently, efforts have been made to standardize operating systems so that software will be compatible across computer brands. The impetus to operating systems development has come from two different sources, hardware vendors and independent software companies. Hardware vendors such as Apple and Radio Shack developed operating systems for their computer hardware. For instance, the DOS (*Disk Operating System*) was developed for the Apple II, SOS (*Sophisticated Operating System*) is used with the Apple III, and the Lisa operating system was created for Apple's top computer.

Software companies, on the other hand, developed operating systems that could be used *across* computer brands, the major ones being CP/M, MS DOS, and Unix. The CP/M operating system, originally an eight-bit processor, was the first and operates on computers such as the DEC Rainbow, Osborne, and specially adapted Apples. Recently they have also developed the CPM 80/86, which is the sixteen-bit version used on the DEC Microcomputers. MS DOS, a sixteen-bit processor, is another operating system competing for the marketplace and is now found on the IBM PC, the DEC Rainbow, and scores of IBM compatible machines. Unix, designed by Bell Laboratories, originally ran on minicomputers and has recently been adapted for micros. For more information on these operating systems, please refer to Figure 4-1 and the box on pp. 46-47.

APPLICATIONS SOFTWARE

Systems software performs tasks for the *machine*—input, processing, output. Applications software consists of programs that perform tasks for the *user*—word processing, accounting, data management. From the users perspective these are the key software packages.

Applications software development has gone through several stages. At the very beginning of the computing era the software was simply given away with the machine's package. If you bought the hardware, certain software was thrown in. As the industry matured and people explored a range of applications, the software industry mushroomed. Software was developed to cover dozens of applications and software costs escalated dramatically. In a large computer installation today the software will frequently cost as much as the hardware. And the combined salaries of programmers and technicians to manage the software can run higher than combined hardware and software costs! Today the software for mainframes and minicomputers is among the most expensive aspects of the whole computer installation.

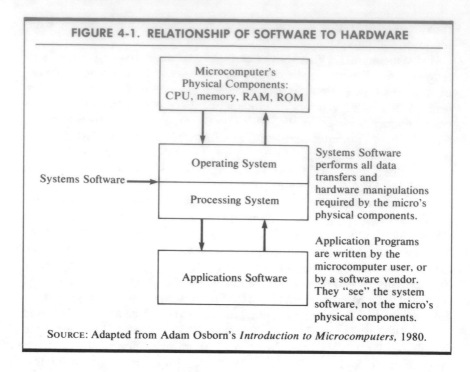

FIGURE 4-1. RELATIONSHIP OF SOFTWARE TO HARDWARE

Microcomputer's Physical Components: CPU, memory, RAM, ROM

Operating System

Systems Software

Processing System

Systems Software performs all data transfers and hardware manipulations required by the micro's physical components.

Applications Software

Application Programs are written by the microcomputer user, or by a software vendor. They "see" the system software, not the micro's physical components.

SOURCE: Adapted from Adam Osborn's *Introduction to Microcomputers,* 1980.

THE OPERATING SYSTEM COMPETITION

Several operating systems are vying for a significant share of the microcomputer marketplace. The primary ones are CP/M, MS-DOS, and Unix. Lisa-style operating systems may soon be contenders.

CP/M: CP/M was the first significant microcomputer operating system. Consequently, it has the largest collection of application software. Because the older microcomputers had limited power, CP/M did not provide sophistication for either developers or users. Updated versions have added concurrency, multi-user capability, and portability. Many of CP/M's features have become de facto standards because of CP/M's popularity on eight-bit computers; however, CP/M is hampered by its limited abilities.

MS-DOS: MS-DOS, designed for the newer sixteen-bit machines, remains largely compatible with the command syntax of CP/M. This has proven to be a winning strategy, and MS-DOS is very successful. At this time MS-DOS runs only on the 8086 microprocessor family. MS-DOS is evolving to resemble Unix more closed by mimicking the tools approach and file structure, which is so useful for program development and applications. MS-DOS has also received a substantial boost because IBM adopted it as the operating system for its PC (calling it PC-DOS for the same system), and now more software is being written in MS-DOS then in any other operating system.

Unix: The Unix operating system, designed by Bell Laboratories ten years ago as a program-development base, originally ran on minicomputers. It is very portable among various machines and has migrated both up and down scale. Though a fine development system, Unix until recently lacked application programs and was not for the end user. It has always provided an integrated, consistent, and powerful environment to software developers through the tools approach. Many observers feel that Unix will soon make a significant move into microcomputers, especially among the more sophisticated lines.

Lisa: The Lisa-style operating system may have a profound effect on the "front-ends" (the interface with the user) of all future operating systems. A Lisa user sees a graphics display with pictorial representations instead of words. He or she operates the system by manipulating a "mouse," a gadget that moves the cursor among the pictures (or "icons"), each of which signifies a command or the data to be handled. In addition, extensive use is made of "windowing," which enables the user to see several displays at once. Other companies are now developing mouse/icon systems, and this approach may see widespread usage.

Other Operating Systems—Apple and Radio Shack: We cannot leave the subject of operating systems without mentioning two old but very popular operating systems. In the early days of the microcomputer revolution—mid to late 1970s—Apple and Radio Shack dominated the field. Each had intentions of being *the* microcomputer company, and each developed a unique operating system which could only run its company's software. Perhaps these companies were so confident of their future dominance that they believed other manufacturers would fall into line and adopt their operating systems. But history proved this overconfidence to be folly, and now Apple and Radio Shack have huge catalogues of eight-bit software that usually work only on their specific machines; there is very little cross-machine compatability. Nevertheless, these two companies have been significant factors in the field, and the software based on their operating systems is extensive and widely used.

With the microcomputer another dramatic development arrived. The applications software is so cheap it is virtually "throw away." For a few thousand dollars the microcomputer user can buy a bag full of software for a dozen different applications, and it will work with sophistication. Why the dramatic shift in price? As long as software manufacturers were producing for mainframes they could expect to sell fifty, one hundred, or maybe a thousand copies of software. With the advent of the microcomputer mass market, however, the software vendors sell to hundreds of thousands of users. Mass marketing allows each piece of software to drop radically in price. The microcomputer software is a whole new ball game. Surprisingly enough, much microcomputer software is nearly as sophisticated as its big siblings with their huge mainframe hosts. The software revolution is as important as the development of the microcomputer itself.

TABLE 4-1. SOFTWARE
Very inexpensive
Whole program costs less than programmer's daily rate
Era of disposable software
Off the shelf availability
Reduces "interval to productivity"—quicker installation
Custom software rarely necessary

The Software Base Is Rapidly Expanding

A few years ago a list of software for the popular microcomputers would fill a few pages. Now the software for Apple computers alone fills a catalog as thick as a big city telephone directory. Most existing software was developed for the older first-generation eight-bit technology but even the new sixteen-bit software is growing by leaps and bounds.

A college or university has many options for useful software. For *managerial* and *office automation* a wealth of software exists for most major machines and for almost any office application as shown in the box on p. 49. For *curriculum uses* the growth of software had been slow but steady, and we anticipate an explosion of educational software in the very near future as more and more educational institutions purchase micro-computers. (We discuss curriculum software in greater detail later in the book.)

For large-scale *administrative purposes* only a handful of programs currently work for such activities as student registration, record keeping, and heavy accounting matters. Most of these administrative functions are still performed by large computers. But an awareness is growing that software will be needed as the microcomputers grow powerful enough to handle these heavy administrative chores.

For *scientific applications* microcomputer software is currently limited, but more is being written every day. For example, social scientists may soon find that microcomputer statistical analysis can supplement the more popular mainframe programs such as SPSS and SAS. In short, a college or university has a wide variety of microcomputer software from which to select. Although the availability varies across applications it is expanding in almost every area. Table 4-1 summarizes some information about applications software.

FUTURE TRENDS IN SOFTWARE

As the machines change the software changes with them. What are the future software developments?

SAMPLE SOFTWARE FOR MANAGERIAL APPLICATIONS

Word Processing: Word processing is the most widely used software program on the microcomputer. This program is simply an electronic editing system that can increase productivity 200 to 300 percent over manual typing. This allows the user to correct mistakes, move word sentences or paragraphs, check spelling, and perform many other tasks.

Mail Lists, Form Letters: The text created in word processing programs can be configured in order to create form letters that will automatically merge with a mailing list to print out hundreds of letters.

Financial Modeling: Financial modeling is possible through the use of electronic spreadsheet programs that can actually replace calculations done formerly with paper, pencil, and calculators. The user creates his own model, after which trend analysis, financial planning, and budgeting can be done instantaneously.

Accounts Payable/Receivable: Accounts receivable allows the user to print invoices, statements, and credit memos. In some programs, the user can define what constitutes column headings on the computer. Accounts payable will print checks, aging reports, cash requirement reports, etc.

General Ledger: These programs usually come with a complete chart of accounts that can be used as is or may be modified to the user's specifications. Data entry is easily accommodated thanks to the program which checks to make sure everything is in balance before posting is allowed.

Business Graphics: A graphics program will create charts and graphs within minutes according to the variables chosen by the user. In addition, color can be obtained by using a color monitor. These graphs can then be printed onto paper using a dot matrix printer or plotter. Slides can be created by photographing the screen with a 35 mm camera.

Data Base Management: DBM systems are electronic filing programs that manage records such as student files, faculty files, or any subject that might presently be on paper files. This system allows the data to be stored, retrieved, and reported in a variety of ways as specified by the user.

Files and Reports: Report programs access information from the data base in order to generate reports that reflect trends and statistical patterns across the entire file. An example report might generate the names, addresses, and phone numbers of all college alumni who donated over $100 last year.

Communications: Communications programs allow the user to send electronic mail or transfer and store large amounts of text from one computer to another. Some programs allow the user to connect to large data base systems, thus providing the user with a vast source of information.

The Cost-Effectiveness of Software Is Increasing

Software cost trends differ from machine cost patterns. The computers have been increasing in capacity and decreasing in price. The software progress has been different: the prices are only gradually coming down, but the capacity increases by leaps and bounds. The increases in cost-effectiveness, then, have generally been on the "effectiveness" side, not always on the "cost" side. However, as the microcomputer business mushrooms into a multi-billion-dollar-a-year activity the competition has become fierce. More and more software houses are being established and prices now seem to be gradually diminishing.

Multiple Functions and Multiple Users Are Now Available in Some Software

Until very recently microcomputer technology allowed one user and one activity at a time. Of course, the software followed suit. With the arrival of the sixteen-bit technology, however, multi-function/multi-user software is now feasible. New operating systems, such a Concurrent CP/M86, support these new multifunction softwares.

Until recently each microcomputer program was devoted to a single purpose. When you bought a software package it would do word processing, or data management, or graphics, or some other single function. With the arrival of sixteen-bit technology, several functions may be integrated into a single software package. For example, the software called Lotus 1,2,3 does budget spreadsheets, simple data base management, and graphics in the same package. Similar "integrated" packages are called Context MBA and Incredible Jack (the latter is written for an eight-bit technology and is not very powerful).

Unfortunately the multiple-task software is still relatively rare and not particularly sophisticated. Usually the combined package is not as powerful as the individual packages that it replaced. However, what they lack in sophistication they gain in convenience and the sophistication of these programs will increase rapidly.

One major convenience is that data prepared for any of the integrated functions can be used in any of the other functions. The same data format is used in all three functions and the programs will "cross-talk" to each other. Contrast this to the previous situation, where each specialized program had its own format. If you had a data base management system and wanted to put information from it into a budget spreadsheet, and then describe the results on a graph, the data had to be completely re-entered three different times into three different programs. If you had an integrated package that incorporated these three functions, you could enter the data one time and do all three functions. This is, of course, a substantial advantage.

Multi-user software is emerging. We mentioned above that multi-user equipment is now being developed from microcomputers. It should be no surprise that the software is following right behind. Figure 4-2 describes the trends in software. Until recently microcomputers have been in the lower left corner of the chart, with single users and single functions. By contrast, large mainframes were in the upper right hand corner

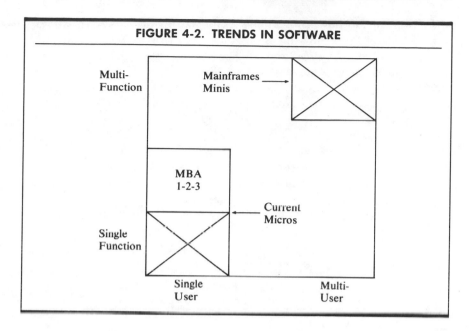

FIGURE 4-2. TRENDS IN SOFTWARE

of the chart, with multiple users and multiple functions simultaneously. The trend will be to move microcomputers out of their limited corner toward the mainframes. Programs like MBA and Lotus 1,2,3 have already moved microcomputers upward along the multiple function axis of the chart.

The Trend toward Universal Operating Systems

One of the biggest frustrations of the microcomputer software world was that software developed for one machine usually did not run on another. The operating system, the software instructions that interfaced the program with the machine, were different from machine to machine. This was an extremely frustrating and expensive problem. If you had more than one kind of machine you simply had to maintain software for each. Often a piece of software that you desperately wanted was configured for the machine you didn't have. Duplication in software and the uselessness of some available software are frustrations generated by mismatched operating systems.

Until very recently there were three operating systems that dominated the microcomputer market. They were the Apple, the Radio Shack TRS-80, and the CP/M operating systems. None of these operating systems interfaced with the others.

Fortunately, there seems to be a slow trend toward more common operating systems. As we mentioned earlier, the day may soon come when most of the popular software will work on almost any machine. The field now seems to have roughly five dominant operating systems: DOS for the Apple System, TRS-DOS for Radio Shack, MS-DOS for the IBM Personal Computer, CP/M, and Unix. On the horizon is one more development, the adaptation of Unix (a leading minicomputer operating system) to the microcomputer field. A trend toward these more common operating systems will be a great benefit for the buyers of microcomputer software.

Rapid Emergence of Educational Software

Much *specialized educational software* is now gradually emerging for microcomputers. Until very recently virtually no educational software was available except on large mainframes and minicomputers. But that scene is changing rapidly, as we shall discuss in detail in Chapter 9.

Before we begin this discussion let us underscore an important point. This chapter and the next are two pieces of the same puzzle: (1) a set of *policy advice* and *criteria* about selecting equipment (this chapter); and (2) recommendations on specific machines that meet the criteria (Chapter 6). *The first part, the policy and criteria discussion, is the most important.* When we mention specific brands in Chapter 6 they are mentioned because *at this moment* they appear to meet the criteria best. But specific brand information changes suddenly—the press each day announces dramatic changes. As these words are being written, for example, the IBM PC Junior is being unveiled on TV. As one prepublication reviewer stated, the advice about brands is probably obsolete before the ink dries. So be it. Thus, the emphasis must be on the *policy issues* and the *criteria* for selection; these will *not* be obsolete even when the brands change radically.

CAMPUS POLICY QUESTIONS ABOUT PURCHASING MICROCOMPUTERS

We believe every campus should decide which microcomputers it will support and which it will help students and faculty to purchase. Some campuses have taken a laissez-faire attitude, leaving the question open for individual departments, faculty, and students. This method leads to madness. In its new book, *The Process of Technological Innovation: Reviewing the Literature* (1983), the National Science Foundation reports that there is a positive correlation between the number of people influencing decisions and the dissatisfaction with the system chosen. In other words, the more people involved in the decision to buy a computer system, the greater the likelihood that the system chosen will have to be modified! Campuses that resist setting a policy or simply resist the general idea of microcomputers find that machines leak in under the doors and through cracks in the windows. We know campuses that tried to establish moratoriums on the purchase of microcomputers while the administrators wrung their hands and thought the issue over. By the time the slow decisions had been made, dozens of brands of microcomputers had sprung up on the campus, resulting in sheer chaos. Consequently, we strongly urge that every campus quickly establish a policy about which microcomputers will be supported and serviced. Not to have a policy is in effect establishing a policy—one of utter confusion.

One Brand per Campus, Two at the Most

We believe most campuses should support one or perhaps two brands of microcomputers. The proliferation of multiple brands will undoubtedly be a mistake and will cause endless headaches. Why do we stress the need for only one or perhaps two brands?

1. The campus will want to maximize expertise and the sharing of knowledge. Having many brands will fragment the base of expertise.
2. Much equipment is *incompatible* across brand lines—printers, disk drives, computers, and monitors for example. To proliferate brands, then, is to cause equipment nightmares.
3. Most software is not compatible across brand lines. Later in the book, we will discuss some attempts to develop uniform software across brands, but such attempts are for the most part in the future. The current situation is that software is brand-specific. To proliferate multiple microcomputer brands is to increase software cost enormously.
4. Data and files are generally machine-specific. Word processing, data base management systems, programming efforts, and other applications where the user creates data are limited to the machine initially used. A multiplicity of brands means that users around campus will not be readily able to share work with other users.
5. Training efforts mounted for faculty, staff, and administrators would have to be tailor-made for each different brand of computer on the campus.
6. Multiple brands make networking machines very difficult. In the future cross-brand networking may be possible, but it is virtually impossible with current technology.
7. To make machines affordable the campus needs the bargaining clout of large purchases to maximize discounts. When everyone goes in different directions the volume is splintered, diminishing the high-volume advantage.

In short, the incompatibility of most equipment and software on today's market suggest that a campus should think about which brand(s) it will support and make a firm policy about it.

The Exception to the "One Brand Only" Rule

Now that we have stated as bluntly as possible the case for one brand of machine, let us back off a little. There are certainly situations that allow a campus to have several brands of microcomputers simultaneously. Although we tend to favor the notion of one brand, we can imagine some campuses selecting several microcomputers for specific reasons. The administrative departments, for example, could conceivably use a brand different from the one used for instructional programs. Engineering departments usually need exceptionally high graphics capabilities. Among the major manufacturers, very few offer this capability (e.g., Hewlett-Packard and DEC) and they may not be the brands selected for general use. So, there are reasons why some people would urge more than one brand of microcomputer on a campus.

On a large campus with highly segregated, highly specialized subunits it may be possible to use multiple brands without total chaos. A large university may find the school of business, the school of engineering, the school of education, and the school of medicine using different machines because of different client and technical demands on the equipment.

Nevertheless, we will still urge that extreme caution be used. We have observed many brands of machines on campuses and have seen much incompatibility. Oftentimes, different officials on the same campus will go and purchase two different brands of microcomputers only to find, too late, that the computers cannot talk to one another. College administrators will have to be extremely firm on this issue, and every department or program chairperson should be pressed to explain why a nonstandard unit should be the exception to the rule. Sometimes this argument will be valid, but in most cases the administrators ought to hold the fort against proliferation of machines. Proliferation increases the cost of both hardware and software, reduces the effects of training, and limits the exchange of expertise on the campus.

HOW TO GET EXPERT ADVICE

Implementing a campus-wide computing program is a difficult task. On the one hand, there is the issue of hardware: which machines to buy, how to network them, and how to plan for the future. On the other hand, there is a complex set of "soft" issues: how to change the curriculum, how to adapt computer literacy into the general education requirements, and how to mount personnel training programs. The decisions on both "hard" and "soft" sides are really quite complex. Even if your campus has an enormous reservoir of expertise, you are going to need expert help. There are at least three major sources of expert help: on-campus experts, hardware vendors, and outside consultants. Let us look at each.

On-Campus Experts

The first place to look for help is, of course, in your own backyard. Most campuses have an impressive array of experts they can tap for very little cost. Most administrators immediately think of the "hard" expertise of the computer science departments and the computer center operations. Administrators should remember, however, that the "soft" issues of curriculum innovation and personnel training are at least as troublesome as the hardware issues. So the first rule is: *From within your own ranks be sure that both "hardware" and "soft issue" people are tapped.*

Your own local people bring many advantages to the table. They are familiar with your computing history and the physical configuration of your current activities. Your own computer experts understand your capabilities and how these mesh with your future plans. Moreover, your own people will have a better sense of budget constraints and realistic options. And, just as important, your own people are going to eventually run the show regardless of the advice that outside vendors or consultants may give you.

Your own people also have strengths on the "soft issues." Remember, the whole purpose is to integrate computing into the larger curriculum. No one is going to know your curriculum and its needs like the people on your campus. Just as important, your local folks are going to know more about the campus political dynamics. Whose toes are being stepped on, what opinion leaders are critical to make this effort succeed, which powerful departments must cooperate before the program is a success? No outsider is going to understand the subtleties of your political environment like the local people do. Nor can an outsider build the strong political support that insures success.

Although your campus people bring many advantages to the table, they also bring many liabilities. It is tempting to try to get expertise inexpensively by using only your local people. For a handful of high-power institutions this will work; but for most colleges and universities a totally inhouse job will most likely have some serious flaws.

To begin with, your "hard" experts are likely to have strong vested interest in the current status quo. After all, they are the priesthood that controls the current religion on your campus. When a new pattern begins to emerge, they might become more of a hindrance than a help. Some computer professionals view the arrival of decentralized computing with microcomputers as a real threat, although this resistance is increasingly rare. Top administrators are well advised to carefully screen the advice coming from their in-house computer professionals. Watch for their potential strong biases.

Outside the priesthood, the new converts on your campus are often devotees of particular machines, or people so entranced with their own patterns of use that they cannot see wider institutional needs. A prepublication reviewer of this book made an important comment at this point:

> Another thing to know about your advisers is where they come from, what *use* they contemplate for the machine. Imagine six people in a room. The first votes for Hewlett-Packard, the second says DEC, the third opts for Apple, the fourth argues for IBM, the fifth insists on Kaypro, the sixth demands Radio Shack. In reality, the first is an engineer thinking graphics, the second an admissions officer thinking word processing, the third is a curriculum specialist, the fourth a guy who just bought Lotus 1,2,3, the fifth a traveling consultant, and the sixth a hobbyist with a machine he got for his kids.

The political involvement of your local people may also be a liability on the "soft" side. It may be helpful to know where the political bones are buried, but your local people might begin fighting the old wars. Some of your local advisers have their own political axes to grind.

In short, your local people are your obvious starting point. As advisers, they bring a world of advantages—they are inexpensive, they know the campus history, they understand your particular curriculum needs, and they are sensitive to the political subleties of the campus fiefdoms. Unfortunately, a number of liabilities come packaged with these advantages. Your local people may have a relatively narrow view of the world. They may be tied up grinding their own political axes, and they may not have enough exposure to alternative arrangements in either computing or curriculum. A wise decision maker would most likely temper the internal advice with some input from the outside world. Where does this external advice come from? Hardware vendors are certainly one major alternative.

Vendors

Hardware manufacturers have one obvious advantage and one obvious disadvantage. On the one hand, their hardware knowledge is generally outstanding. On the other hand, they have a vested interest in giving you a biased opinion. The problem for the administrator is as old as the hills: how can you pick the hardware manufacturer's brains without getting snookered?

Incidentally, let us pause a second and look back at another bias problem. When you think about the hardware manufacturers, the question of vested interest and bias immediately leaps to your mind. But most of us are not as on-guard when we confront our own campus advisers. Why not? They probably have just as many reasons to give you provincial and biased opinions as an outside hardware vendor. Your computer center director's job is on the line, his or her budget is at stake, his or her status in the organization must be protected. A new convert may have a strong bias for a particular machine because he or she owns one and does not want the campus to buy incompatible equipment. Why are we not just as suspicious of the biased motives of our own people as we are of outsiders? This is not necessarily a cynical view; rather it is an attempt to illustrate an obvious point.

What can we do with the hardware vendors? How can we gather the roses without necessarily being led down the garden path? Here are a few ideas.

First, give the hardware manufacturers a chance to educate you. As obvious as this may seem, we have seen many situations where people are so afraid to be tainted by sales pitches that they maintain too great a distance to learn anything. The hardware manufacturers actually are the experts on their equipment. They are usually eager to give a full explanation and a great deal of help. However, our experience is that hardware vendors rarely get a chance to begin teaching the colleges what they know because the decision makers simply will not take the time to listen. This is a tragedy, because the vendors are a fabulous source of information. We have found that the top vendors are extremely ethical in their presentations—if not because of sterling ethics then because they don't want to live with lies later!

Second, it pays to listen to a number of vendors, not just the one you're familiar with. The field changes rapidly, and different vendors have different things to offer. Moreover, there are enormous differences in pricing, service, and willingness to advise your campus. So do check around. Comparison shopping pays in this field, too. By hearing full presentations from a variety of vendors, you can glean enormous amounts of helpful advice.

Consultants as a Source of Advice

If chosen wisely, consultants can, in fact, be a relatively inexpensive way to get advice. This does not necessarily mean that their dollar cost is low. However, if consultants save you from a serious mistake in this complex and expensive arena, their advice is certainly cost effective. Consultants are at an obvious disadvantage in some areas. They are not as familiar with your campus as your own people are. They do not know your curriculum intimately and have virtually no knowledge of the politics in your kingdom. Moreover, most consultants do not know as much about equipment as hardware vendors. Nevertheless, in spite of these disadvantages, consultants can offer many strengths.

First, a consultant can serve as a counterbalance to the built-in biases and political positions of your in-house people. For example, a seasoned consultant can speak with the authority necessary to balance your own computer professionals. The consultant may be blind to your own in-house political consideration, and as a consequence, may often make terrible blunders. Under other circumstances, however, this can be a tremendous advantage. Who else but a politically blind consultant is likely to declare that the emperors in your particular empire have no clothes? Of course, there is a fine line here. You don't need Attila the Hun as your consultant blundering around the campus dispensing *faux pas* in every direction. But a little refreshing naiveté can be a valuable commodity in a good consultant.

Second, the experienced consultant can tell you what other folks are doing. One of the most desired services of a consultant is the airing of new ideas. A consultant who has "been around the block" can impart many fresh ideas in a very short time. So, the first pieces of information to obtain from a consultant should be what other campuses are doing, what has worked elsewhere, and where problems occurred.

Third, a good consultant is organized and prepared to handle training issues. Undoubtedly, your in-house people could conduct training programs for faculty. But how long does it take to prepare for those training programs? How much time-lag can your campus afford? How expensive is it to pull existing personnel off their regular tasks? Campuses generally have people that already know about computers and microcomputers. Unfortunately, these people are not readily organized to conduct effective training programs. It is both time-consuming and expensive for in-house people to tool up for such a task. An experienced consultant can move in rapidly, do the job, and, in the long run, save the campus money. A seasoned consultant is simply better prepared for such advising tasks.

Fourth, an experienced consultant can help you balance the competing claims of the hardware vendors. Some consultants have connections with hardware vendors. These ties are either financial or consist simply of a pattern of doing business with a vendor with whom they feel comfortable. The consultant-vendor connection is no cause for alarm. In fact, much good can result from the relationship such as unusually good discounts. It is important to determine what the relationship is between the consultant and the vendor, and to balance it carefully in the decision-making process.

Most of the consultants in the field have some kind of connection with the manufacturers. It is likely that the consultant has worked closely with a certain vendor. The consultant has probably been educated and aided by that manufacturer. Therefore, a prejudice in favor of that vendor has been established. This poses no problem as long as these biases are clearly stated and the consultant's advice—along with the other parties around the table—is taken with a hefty grain of salt.

This leads to one final point about consultants. Because they have had close working relationships with a vendor, some consultants are able to obtain favorable discounts. These discounts are clearly above and beyond what the company normally would give. You may find that the consultant–company relationship actually pays for the consulting advice. We have seen many cases where the consultants were able to obtain such substantial discounts that their services, in effect, were completely free to the colleges.

Where Do You Hunt for an Appropriate Consultant?

You know where to go for your on-campus advice, and the hardware vendors are clearly established. But where do you find a good consultant? Here are a few suggestions:

1. Ask the hardware vendors to suggest consultants.
2. Check with EDUCOM, a national association for advancing computers in colleges.
3. Contact the authors of this book at the Graduate School of Education at UCLA.
4. Inquire from CAUSE in Boulder, Colorado, an organization that has dealt with campus computing problems.
5. Write or call some of the campuses that appear to have programs similar to the one you wish to establish.
6. Several colleges of education have faculty that have strong interests in college-level microcomputing, including Stanford, Teacher's College at Columbia, and Ohio State.

Any of the suggestions above are likely to uncover a number of consultants.

From the discussion above it is clear that some *combination* of advice is needed. Inside experts, manufacturers of equipment, and consultants can all contribute to your program. A thoughtful administrator will obtain advice from all three options.

CRITERIA FOR SELECTING MICROCOMPUTERS

Everybody has their favorite machine. Microcomputers are like good scotch; when you're hooked on one brand, you won't change easily. Everybody can mount an impassioned argument why their particular brand is the best. "My machine has more memory, more storage, is CP/M compatible, and has a better keyboard." Ah, but the retort is just as vigorous: "But my machine is a sixteen-bit processor, comes with dual disk drives, and has a high resolution monitor!"

Most of these arguments miss the point. They focus almost exclusively on the *machine characteristics*. Certainly machine characteristics are important, but there is an entire range of other factors that must be carefully considered. These factors often tip the scale where machine characteristics do not. Look at Table 5-1. We have listed five criteria: (1)

TABLE 5-1. CRITERIA FOR SELECTING A MICROCOMPUTER

1. Machine generation
2. Widespread use
3. Software availability and compatibility
4. Support and service
5. Cost
    basic equipment
    peripherals
    software
    supplies
    maintenance

machine generation; (2) widespread use; (3) software; (4) service availability; and (5) cost. This is the general principle: *campuses have to review these competing criteria and find the machine that best balances them*. Unfortunately, there is no absolute winner that places high on all five criteria. When all is said and done, for the college market, only three companies produce machines that rate significantly high on the *combined* set of criteria: Apple, IBM, and DEC. We will explain why we prefer these machines later, but first let us examine the set of criteria in more detail.

Machine Generation

Chapter 3 explained the three generations of microcomputers. The first-generation machines, from the late 1970s, usually had small memory, forty-column screens, very limited storage capacity, and poor keyboards. These machines still exist. Most of the less expensive "home" computers made by Atari, Sinclair, Commodore, and Timex fall within the first-generation group. Not too many circumstances would justify a campus purchasing a first-generation machine. The Apple II was the only one widely used on campuses. Since the upgraded Apple IIe is now available, no one should consider purchasing the Apple II. First-generation machines are much too limited for serious college work and should be scratched from the list.

The second-generation machines had more memory, upgraded keyboards, larger storage capacity, and other special features. However, they generally used an eight-bit processor, a remnant of the first generation thus limiting the degree of sophistication in the software. The Apple IIe, Apple III, the Franklin, and numerous other machines would fit into this second-generation machine category.

The third-generation machines were upgraded further. The major distinguishing feature of this new generation is the use of a sixteen-bit processor that allows for more sophisticated software.

The general rule is that a college ought to select equipment from the most advanced generation of machines. However, consideration of a second-generation machine is possible—if other criteria compel the decision. The Apple IIe or the Apple III are the only second-generation machines that score high enough on the other criteria to be possible contenders. Campuses should focus on third-generation machines, with the exception of the Apple IIe and III. There are no situations where a first-generation machine would be advisable on a college campus.

We want to emphasize this point: *campuses should be buying high-quality, third-generation machines* (with the possible exception of the two Apple machines, which we will explain shortly). Too many campuses have fallen for the "more is better" hypothesis, have bought cheap, older-generation machines, and have lived to regret it. The less powerful, older-generation machines simply do not have the sophistication needed for serious, college-level computing. Too many colleges, concentrating on cost alone, have squandered money on machines that simply have no power, no adequate software, and no advanced features. Specifically:

- they cannot be easily networked;
- they cannot use the newer generation of multi-task, multi-user software;
- they do not have high-quality graphics;
- they cannot be used in conjunction with interactive video (see Chapter 8 for a discussion of this point);
- they do not have enough internal memory for serious work;
- they are often woefully inadequate in their disk storage capacities, thus prohibiting important applications (such as large files or large data bases).

Third-generation machines by contrast usually have advanced features that overcome these problems. We cannot emphasize this point enough: buy quality, buy upward growth, buy for the future as much as possible. It seems most imperative now, at the beginning of the microcomputer revolution, to get machines into people's hands. But shortly we will face more important issues: what can we *do* with these machines? The next generation of students coming out of high school will have cut their teeth on simple machines and will be hungry for more meat in their intellectual and computer diet. The fever to buy inexpensive machines will rapidly give way to frustrated disappointment when the unsophisticated machines do not fulfill the need for powerful, networked microcomputers in integrated campus frameworks doing serious computing.

We believe that the "buy sophistication" rule is even more reasonable when it becomes apparent that the cost between machines is not so great when all costs are considered. We will return shortly to this cost issue.

Widespread Use

The machine is definitely a baseline consideration. If it were the only factor, at least twentyfive or thirty machines would merit careful consideration. However, user context, the second criterion, eliminates most of these twentyfive or thirty good machines.

There are many pieces to the puzzle that makes up an effective campus computer program. The machine is only one piece; the user context is another—and just as important. What do we mean by user context? The concept is quite simple. It refers to what other people are using—both on your local campus and at the national education level. Enormous advantages accompany a widespread machine with many users. There is vast user expertise, and a wealth of practical information about what does and does not work. Also, it is easier to find out how to make things happen, where to get software, and how to use it. In addition, a widely used machine has a snowballing effect on software.

Having a large user base is a distinct advantage because of the proliferation of equipment accessories. Machines that are widely used promote a "third-party" equipment industry. Interesting and useful accessories will be developed if the machine has a large enough installation base to justify it. For example, hard disk drives, which allow for mass storage, are available only for the most popular machines. The same is true of such handy items as graphics tables, specialized plotters, scientific metering devices, and (very important for educators) special teaching devices such as interactive video equipment.

In short, the user context is one of the single most important issues in selecting a microcomputer. Again, the user base is another factor underscoring our basic rule—"stay mainline."

Software Availability

In the computer industry, the software separates the sheep from the goats. Many companies have excellent machines. The sad truth is that only the "mainline" machines have a wide variety of software. Any time you consider buying a microcomputer, you should consider the software issue carefully—*very carefully*.

Many colleges make costly mistakes when equipping themselves for the computer age. David Marker, provost of Hope College, said that Hope had "done it wrong twice" (Magarrell, 1983e). In the 1960s and 1970s, Hope College's faculty members went shopping for hardware for the campus—but in the wrong way. As Dr. Marker puts it, "they were shopping for hardware comparing brands and models, like people shopping for a car." Finally, the third time, the college followed the rules.

They studied what kind of computer jobs needed doing, found software programs to do those jobs, and then selected the hardware that would efficiently run the selected software. If you are interested in a large institutional purchase, demand that any off-brand machine you are considering (against our advice!) has a *demonstration* of the software you will need. There are several rules to consider about the software issue.

First, you should buy a microcomputer that has a large software base. However, this should not simply be measured as a number of titles in the software library. Among the sixteen-bit machines, the software library may be relatively small, but the available programs may be quite sophisticated. Apple, IBM, and DEC—the companies we recommend—have large software bases.

Next are the standard operating systems. It used to be that each company had a unique operating system. Software from one machine would not run on another. In recent years, however, two software systems have made strong efforts to become the industry standards: CP/M and MS/DOS. CP/M probably has more software, whereas MS/DOS is probably more sophisticated. As CP/M and MS/DOS expand, accessibility to the huge base of software will also expand. This is a distinct advantage for the "off-brand" companies. Their microcomputers can now utilize CP/M or MS/DOS software written for the mainline companies. This may mean that the off-brand companies will someday have a fighting chance to claim your attention after all!

However, before you run out and buy a CP/M or MS/DOS compatible off-brand machine you should be cautioned. This new software rarely works by simply plugging it in. Even when the software uses a standardized operating system, the programs usually require a modification. This is due to differences in keyboards, disk drive configurations, and other factors which differ from machine to machine. In short, the era of completely standardized software is still a promise, not a reality. So, be sure to judge all software claims with a suspicious eye, and demand to see a standard copy of software running on the machine you chose.

Finally, you should look into the software base available for any specific unique needs. For example, if you want standard educational programs for remedial education, you're almost limited to Apple. If networking a larger minicomputer is a critical issue, make sure the machine you are considering has advanced networking capabilities, such as the DEC. In general, the three companies we recommend have a large base of specific-need software. In fact, the largest companies actively work with software vendors to promote specialized software—another reason to stay mainline. Once you get off the mainline, you may have a difficult time covering your specific software needs. Incidentally, in the area of specialized needs Hewlett-Packard might be given serious consideration because it has specialized software for engineers and scientists.

Service

The *electronic* components of a microcomputer, such as the central processing unit, generally are not prone to service problems. However, the *mechanical accessories* are notorious for breaking down. Printers and disk drives can be a real pain in the neck! Software will often need a particular kind of service, namely, advice on how to make it work! Where do you get service when you need it?

The first rule of thumb is to buy equipment only from a company with service centers in your immediate area. *Do not* buy from a dealer or a company that is far away and promises they will send somebody to fix any problem. Those promises are not worth the hot air they're spoken with. You need somebody local, somebody with a serious service center, and somebody who will snap to when you need help. This is another reason why we emphasize the "stay mainline" maxim.

Be Aware of Service Contract Pitfalls

Some service contracts promise quick service. In fact, some are even written in terms of the number of hours it takes for the service man to appear—four hours, twentyfour hours, or some other specific time. These "speedy clauses" do not mean much in reality. How do you handle the capriciousness of service contracts? In addition to screaming, there are some other steps you can take.

Most major manufacturers will train your people in routine maintenance and service. You should definitely take advantage of this opportunity. It will save you a lot of money in the long run.

You will want some healthy redundancy in your system. Because you cannot depend on instantaneous service, you will want to have a few extra pieces of equipment around such as disk drives and printers, since they are the most trouble-prone. Although equipment redundancy may seem a little expensive, it is one way to be sure you always have equipment up and running. The need for redundancy reinforces the advice to stick with one brand of machine. The proliferation of different brands of machines around the campus make establishing redundancies extremely difficult. With one brand of machine throughout the campus you have a built-in redundancy that is very cost-effective.

What about service contracts? Some campuses establish elaborate service contracts with the manufacturer as they do on all their other equipment. Other campuses depend on drop-in service to their local dealer along with some on-site training for their own people. Since microcomputers are so portable, it is feasible that a local service center on your campus can handle many of the smaller problems. Larger problems can be taken to your local area dealer. It is clearly more expensive to opt for the service contracts, and several campuses have gotten along well without them.

Cost

In spite of what the ads say, microcomputers of the second and third generation vary in price within a rather narrow range. Most of the inexpensive machines fall into the first-generation category. At both the second- and third-generation levels, it is quite surprising to find that the *total* cost of the machines and all their peripherals vary only slightly. Most purchasers are fooled by examining only the central processing unit in the cost equation. The CPUs do vary substantially—from $1,000 to $2,000. This may look like a 100 percent difference in price, but this is misleading. When you consider the disk drives, the software, the monitors, and the printers, the *total* difference in cost for similarly configured machines is not so large, as you can see from Table 7-2 in Chapter 7. Be sure that your figures are based on the total cost. Most people are shocked to find, for example, that printers often cost more than the microcomputers. First, figure out the basic configuration of equipment you want to price, then demand that everybody give you comparable bids.

Let's take the "total cost" concept a little further. Our argument is simple: if you take all costs into consideration the difference between "inexpensive" and "expensive" microcomputers is not worth sacrificing the sophistication and company support that goes with the mainline brand. Suppose you want to install a laboratory with twenty-four machines. In Chapter 7 we propose such a lab and calculate its cost. The bottom-line difference between a program based on high-quality equipment and "cheap" equipment is 38 percent. We do not believe such savings justify low-performance machines as the keystone of your program.

There are only a couple of ways to buy machines inexpensively. On the one hand, you can succumb to temptation and buy a first-generation machine—an Atari, a Commodore, or a Sinclair. We feel, as you know, that this is madness for a serious college campus! Until those machines

TABLE 5-2. COST COMPARISONS

	"Expensive"	"Inexpensive"	Percent Difference
Equipment	$ 50,000	$ 30,000	66
Training	12,000	12,000	0
Software	5,000	5,000	0
Remodeling for lab	5,000	5,000	0
Total	$ 72,000	$ 52,000	38

are upgraded substantially, they should not be the centerpiece of your campus computer programs. On the other hand, you can risk buying some of the "look-alikes," such as the Franklin or some of the IBM clones. But this risk saves you very little when you consider the *total* cost of the machine and all its peripherals. Both of these strategies to save money—the inexpensive first-generation machines and the look-alikes—are penny-wise-and-pound-foolish in the long run.

A much better way to save money is to approach the mainline manufacturers and press hard for discounts. Without exceptions, all of them will give educational institutions substantial price breaks. You are best advised to spend your time haggling with the major manufacturers than wandering into the woods trying to buy an off-brand lower-priced machine.

Combining the Criteria

A decision to select a machine must take into account *all* of the above factors. Machine characteristics are the focal point for most people, but this is only a portion of the puzzle. The user context, software, service, and cost are also important pieces. Considering all of these factors, we think the leading microcomputer contenders for campus use come from only four companies. The next chapter looks at these four.

CHAPTER 6

OUR

FAVORITE MACHINES

This chapter will undoubtedly upset some readers. We will talk about how various companies meet the criteria we outlined above, and we will then recommend four specific brands for purchase. In all of our training workshops, this "which machine to buy" decision is always the most spirited. We displease at least half the crowd because their preferred brand does not get recommended. We hate to upset people but we think some very concrete advice about brand issues is critical. At last count, there were over 150 brands of microcomputers on the market. For us to duck the question of brand evaluation would be irresponsible. We have already specified some criteria; we will now explain what machines we think meet those criteria. Readers can change the criteria if they desire and they might even come up with other brands that meet the test. We feel we must provoke the conversation because millions of dollars will be spent and there ought to be some rationale behind those expenditures.

Which microcomputers on the market are the best choices according to the criteria? Now we enter the thicket! Everybody has an idea about which machines are best. We have learned that it is easier to criticize the American flag than somebody's brand of microcomputer. But we are going to take the plunge. As of the end of 1983, we think that colleges would be wise to buy machines from one of four companies: Apple, International Business Machines (IBM), the Digital Equipment Company (DEC), and Hewlett-Packard (HP). These companies not only produce excellent equipment, they also have targeted higher education as a key market and as an area of support.

There will undoubtedly be some people who would suggest other brands. There are certainly other excellent machines out there. Remember, we are not only talking about machines; *we are talking about an entire range of criteria*. We insist that issues such as user context, software availability, and investment in education are all as legitimate as machine sophistication. If we were only judging *machine* characteristics, there would be dozens of companies we could recommend. When all of these factors are considered, however, Apple, IBM, DEC, and HP get our votes. Let us explain why.

OUR CHOICES

The Apple Series of Microcomputers

The Apple line of products is very broad. At this point, the only machine widely used in education is the Apple II and its enhanced sister, the Apple IIe. But the new MacIntosh looks very promising. We will discuss the Mac in a moment, but in passing it might be reasonable for some colleges, especially those with heavy teacher-education emphasis, to consider continuing to buy the Apple IIe.

A reasonable person might ask why one would want to buy a second-generation machine when there are excellent third-generation machines available. The answer is simple. The Apple IIe does not win on machine characteristics but on other points: the enormous availability of software, the staggering user base, and a long-time interest in and support of elementary and secondary education. These are important points, not to be viewed lightly. Apple is a major force in education, both elementary-secondary and higher education. Computer-assisted instruction packages have almost always been configured for the Apple first. In addition, the software base for noneducational purposes is the largest in the microcomputer industry, although most of it is the older eight-bit technology. Whatever you desire in software, Apple IIe is almost sure to have it. In short, the Apple IIe product line is included in our "recommended" list because of widespread use and software issues. The IIe machine is acceptable although not state-of-the-art, especially for teacher-education programs.

What about other Apple products more advanced than the IIe? The III is actually a second-generation machine. It has an improved keyboard, upgraded memory, a ten-key pad, and some more sophisticated software. But it is still an eight-bit processor, so it cannot be considered as a member of the third generation. In addition, Apple made some marketing errors and the machine never became as successful as the Apple II series. Nevertheless, the machine is excellent, runs most Apple II series software, and should be seriously considered among campus possibilities. Actually, it costs very little more than the IIe when all costs are considered, and it is probably more cost-effective, offering more machine per dollar spent.

Apple's top entry into the microcomputer market is the expensive and powerful "Lisa." The Lisa uses an extremely advanced micro chip and has enormous built-in memory—500K. It also runs a new, sophisticated software that is integrated with a number of uses. The programs are directed by a "mouse," a mechanical gadget that directs screen activity and alleviates the user having to learn most commands. The technology and software on the Lisa are indeed impressive. Unfortunately, as this book is being written, about the only software that will run on Lisa is the package that is included with the machine, although Apple is actively promoting additional software development. If Lisa becomes popular, undoubtedly more software will be written. At the moment, Lisa cannot run the older Apple II and III software, and only limited software has been written for the machine. This is a serious set of liabilities. In addition, the price tag—about $8000 in early 1984—puts it out of most campuses' reach. However, as production and sales gear up the Lisa price could fall much further, making it a machine to watch.

On January 24, 1984, Apple introduced its newest product, the MacIntosh. The MacIntosh is a 32-bit machine with 128K RAM and a single built-in disk drive. The entire unit—monitor, keyboard, and CPU—weighs slightly over 20 pounds and covers about one square foot of desk top. The MacIntosh employs the "Lisa" technology—point with a mouse, click, pull down menus. Mac intends to be compatible with some Lisa software.

MacIntosh should be a very attractive machine for colleges and universities. Indeed, Apple made special efforts to promote the machine among leading colleges and universities. Before announcing the product to the public, Apple signed agreements with twenty-four institutions. They agreed to buy large quantities, and Apple agreed to give substantial discounts.

Different companies have used different techniques to handle the interface between the user and the machine. Hewlett-Packard has developed a touch screen; Digital has the industry's most sophisticated keyboard with special keys to simplify interface; Apple has chosen the mouse as its interface solution. All of these are excellent solutions; some people may prefer one over the other. The touch screen, the elaborate keyboard, and the mouse are all reasonable solutions to the same machine/human interface problem. Apple is betting on the mouse, a small control device that sits beside the keyboard. The mouse is especially attactive for first-time unsophisticated users. (More experienced users may actually not like a mouse, and may prefer to work more with the keyboard where they do not have to move back and forth between the mouse and the keyboard.) The MacIntosh mouse replaces many of the command codes that normally run a computer. The mouse has a pointer; the user points to various command sequences and leads the machine through the various activities. For some people this technique is easier than using a keyboard.

With any new machine software availability is a major concern.

Apple was hurt badly by the lack of software on its high-priced Lisa, MacIntosh's big sister. The company was determined not to get burned again, so they seeded MacIntosh machines to many software vendors long before it was available to the public. Apple claims there will be 500 programs in the first year; allowing for overstatement it seems reasonable to expect 50 to 150. Sales of the new machine have been brisk even though it had very little software at introduction; these sales will in turn promote more software development.

MacIntosh should be popular on college campuses. It is light, and has a nylon carrying case that handles the whole unit. Moreover, Apple's aggressive pricing for colleges and universities should further heighten interest in the product. The employees and students at the twenty-four Apple Consortium institutions were able to buy the machine for about $1,000. However, we have mentioned that pricing is sometimes slippery, and if one adds the price of a second disk drive and a printer, the real price will be just under $2,000—about the same as the DEC Rainbow, the IBM PC, and the HP 150 after discounts are figured in. The price competetion between Apple, DEC, and IBM should heat up, reducing the average price even on campuses that have not been part of the Big Three's special discounting arrangements.

The MacIntosh may be a winner. Unlike the other recent Apple low-selling products (Lisa and Apple III), MacIntosh may be the successful replacement of the old workhorse Apple II. Mac has excellent graphics (regrettably not in color) and the mouse technology, which may be highly favored by first-time unsophisticated users—the market that Mac is targeting. The machine is off to a good start on college campuses. Clearly MacIntosh is a machine to watch.

The IBM Personal Computer

IBM is the largest computer company in the world. When IBM makes a move in the computer world, the reverberations are felt everywhere. This was certainly the case with IBM's introduction of its personal computer (PC).

IBM introduced the PC as a true third-generation microcomputer. It has both an eight-bit and sixteen-bit processor, substantial memory and storage, and the full weight of IBM's massive company behind it. It is no surprise that the PC had instantaneous success. Although IBM is not revealing the volume of sales, the level of excitement about the PC is apparent from the magazines that focus on it exclusively. *PC World* and *PC Magazine* started out as slim volumes but quickly grew to the size of a good-size telephone directory! If IBM has not already caught up with the Apple as the number one selling microcomputer company, then it certainly cannot be far behind.

When we run the PC through our judgment criteria it does extremely well. The machine is among the better on the market, clearly the sales leader of the third-generation microcomputers. In addition, software is being written for it at an astonishing rate. Three years ago almost all software vendors thought of Apple first for their market. But today most software vendors are probably writing more for the PC than anything else.

Where are IBM's soft spots? There are only two weaknesses and frankly they are not overwhelming. First, the IBM PC costs roughly $2,000 more than a similarly configured Apple IIe. In addition, very little educational software has been written for the PC. However, later we will discuss that we do not think very highly of the available education software anyway, so this may not be a major liability. Certainly, there is a full range of high-quality software written for noneducational purposes. Many of these can be adapted to an educational role. We do not think that the absence of specific educational software is a dramatic barrier to purchasing the IBM PC.

In short, if the college is willing to invest the additional cash, the IBM PC is a strong contender in a campus computer program. Carnegie-Mellon, for example, adopted the PC into its campus-wide computer effort.

The newest IBM product, the IBM PCjr, offers yet another option to the confusing array of computer products. The standard memory size is 64K, upgradable to 128K. Its microprocessor is the same one used in the IBM PC. However, some software may require special alterations due to a slightly different operating system in the PCjr. The amount of real compatibility with the PC is an unproven issue. An intriguing feature is the cordless infrared keyboard that allows the user to enter information with the keyboard while standing approximately 20 feet from the CPU. The upgraded PCjr also can use both cartridge and diskette-based software. Presently, a PCjr with disk drive, 64K, and a monitor costs nearly $2,000. A comparable Apple IIe system can be purchased for $1,600 retail.

What does this mean for the college administrator who must decide what computer system to buy? In our view, nothing has changed significantly. Our recommendation is still to buy the sophisticated, mainline, upgradable machine.

One prepublication reviewer wanted to know why we would advise the Apple IIe, but not the PCjr? Our main reason for recommending the Apple IIe is not the sophistication or upward potential of the machine. Rather, Apple IIe has the most extensive educational software base of any other computer system. A sophisticated machine is of no use if it cannot run the programs needed by the user. Although the PCjr may run some of the PC software, the educational software base for the PC is not particularly impressive. Will more educational software be written for the PCjr in hopes of capturing the educational market? Probably. But until then, the Apple IIe system can do much more and costs less.

The DEC Line of Microcomputers

The Digital Equipment Company is the second largest computer company in the world. Although it does not have the instant name recognition that Apple and IBM have with the general public, DEC is a well-known company among computer experts and campus administrators. DEC made enormous inroads into campus computing activities with their excellent line of minicomputers: the PDP-11 and VAX series. In fact, DEC believes they have more installed minicomputers on campuses than any other company. The PDP's and the VAX's have been extraordinarily popular as middle-sized computers, and are the work horses on many American campuses.

DEC was a bit late entering the microcomputer business. But when it did jump into the fray, it produced three outstanding products. The Rainbow is DEC's bid into the third-generation general-purpose microcomputer group; the Decmate II is a very cost-effective word processor; and the Professional 300 series is a very sophisticated upper-level microcomputer. In reality, the Professional could claim the power and sophistication of a minicomputer. All three machines are exceptionally sophisticated and technically are probably the best among the third-generation microcomputers.

The Rainbow is likely to be the most widely used of DEC's microcomputers. It compares favorably with the IBM PC, and many people argue that it is more sophisticated. Like the IBM, the Rainbow has a dual eight-bit and a sixteen-bit processor built in. This means that both the Rainbow and the IBM can run the older eight-bit software and the newer sixteen-bit programs. This dual capacity is a very smart idea since the old eight-bit software still dominates the market.

The Decmate II is an excellent, cost-effective word processing machine, and can be quite useful in campus office automation. The Professional 300 series is a sophisticated cross between a microcomputer and a minicomputer. It actually contains a microprocessor from the PDP series of minicomputers. Most likely, the Professional will be popular among campuses with strong scientific and engineering applications. Unfortunately, most of the common sixteen-bit microcomputer software will not run on the Professional. It requires the minicomputer software from the PDP series. However, a card inserted into the machine will enable it to run older eight-bit software. Most campuses that adopt a Professional do so because of high-level scientific and engineering work. Although the Professional is an excellent machine, the Rainbow will probably be more popular as an all-purpose campus microcomputer.

The DEC series scores highly with us because of its *networking* capabilities. As more and more microcomputers are put onto campuses there will be a strong demand for networking capabilities. They will either be "local area networks" among a group of microcomputers or "mainframe networks" linking microcomputers to larger equipment.

DEC has been a leader in the networking area. The company has an enormous base of minicomputers installed on campuses, and is aggressively working to link its microcomputer series with its minicomputers. DEC has more expertise in networking issues than most companies. They have developed a sophisticated networking capability known as DECNET. The DECNET system is extremely efficient, especially when the on-line equipment is also from DEC. Since many colleges have DEC minicomputers, one may be well advised to consider DEC microcomputers.

In short, the DEC microcomputers have some obvious strengths. They offer more variety in their microcomputer series, including the extremely sophisticated Professional 300 model which is actually a minicomputer; their microcomputers are technically excellent; DEC probably has more current networking capability for microcomputers than any other company; and DEC microcomputers are roughly in the same price range as IBM's PC.

DEC's weaknesses stem largely from their late entry into the microcomputer market. Since DEC has offered microcomputers for only a short time, the company is well behind both Apple and IBM in terms of sales. This fact results in two negative impacts. First, the user context is, by definition, smaller. You will not be able to find as many people with Rainbows. Consequently, it will be more difficult to share expertise and learning. Second, because DEC microcomputers have existed for only a short time, there was until recently a shortage of available software. However, DEC has now overcome that problem, and at the end of 1983 over 600 programs were offered, most in the newer sixteen-bit format. Almost all the important software programs are now available. Moreover, the machine has both the popular CP/M operating system and MS-DOS, another common operating system used by IBM's PC, for which there is much available software. We expect the Rainbow to be a very popular microcomputer, especially on campuses that already have DEC minicomputers that can be networked with the micros.

The Hewlett-Packard Line

Our fourth and final favorite is the Hewlett-Packard (HP) line. You might wonder why we recommend this line when HP's newest microcomputer, the HP150, is brand new and thus far unproven.

First of all, we feel that the strength of the company warrants some serious consideration of their microcomputer. For years HP has produced high-quality products. Hewlett-Packard has long been involved with colleges and universities as an outstanding manufacturer of high-performance products in the fields of science and engineering.

The HP 3000 series minicomputer has been extremely popular. According to Computer Intelligence Corporation, this minicomputer has the second largest nationally installed base of general purpose computers, second only to the IBM System/34. And HP's academic presence is strong, with the third largest base of minicomputers after DEC and IBM.

As for their microcomputers, the HP85, a 64K machine, was an early engineering and technical product. Following close behind were the HP120 and HP125 models. These two microcomputers have eight-bit processors and run CP/M software. However, they are more technically oriented and never have been very popular in education outside of science and engineering. These two microcomputers did not make much of an impression on general computing in colleges and universities.

Two other microcomputers made by HP deserve mention: the HP200 model 16 and the HP 9000 series. Although we feel these micros are too specialized and probably too expensive for the general needs of higher education, you should know they exist. The HP200 is an extremely sophisticated machine geared for engineering and runs $7,500 and up. The HP9000 series is a dedicated thirtytwo-bit desk top computer for the single user, so powerful it is called "a mainframe in a box." It has a two-megabyte storage capacity and costs about $27,000.

For general purpose computing at the higher education level, however, HP brings to the microcomputer market a serious new competitor: the HP150. This microcomputer introduces an interesting idea—the touch-sensitive screen. Although touch screens have been around for years, this is the first major use in a microcomputer series. HP figures that people naturally point at what they want. This touch screen allows users to do just that. In "HPTouch," commands, cursor movement, and data movement are all accomplished by a simple touch of the screen.

It's not just the touch-sensitive screen that makes the new microcomputer impressive. Rather, the machine's sophistication and ease of use give the machine its appeal. The HP150 standard system has a sixteen bit (8088) processor, 256K memory, MS-DOS operating system, and dual floppy disk drives set in a very compact hardware arrangement. Memory and mass storage capacity of the HP150 is equivalent to the IBM PC and the DEC Rainbow, fully configured. The HP150 runs roughly $4,000 retail, slightly more than the IBM and the DEC Rainbow. Of course, retail price is no indication of how much it would cost a college or university. As yet, HP has not announced any special discounts, but negotiations would surely yield some results.

What about the software base? The HP150 uses MS-DOS, and scores of programs are available. Although starting late, HP should have no serious problem with software availability.

Should colleges and universities seriously consider the HP150, a Johnny-come-lately to the market? That depends on many factors. First, how valuable will the touch screen turn out to be? Will it reduce learning time? Second, does the institution already have HP minicomputers that can serve as the hub of networks? This is a very serious consideration, as we mentioned in discussing the DEC line. The choice depends on these

	DEC Rainbow	Apple MacIntosh	IBM PC	HP150
Machine generation	Excellent	Excellent	Excellent	Excellent
Widespread user base	Good	Fair	Excellent	Fair
Software	Excellent	Poor/ Fair	Excellent	Good
Obsolescence	Excellent	Excellent	Excellent	Excellent
Service	Excellent	Excellent	Excellent	Excellent
Cost	Good	Good	Good	Good

Table title: TABLE 6-1. RATING FOUR MICRO'S

and other questions, but we suspect colleges will want to consider the HP line seriously in spite of its late entry into the market.

The Brands Compared

Table 6-1 compares the machines that pass our criteria test. No machine is perfect, but these rate high enough overall for us to have a clear conscience in suggesting their use. The DEC equipment is seemingly the most technically sophisticated. Apple certainly has the largest user base, software base, and educational background. IBM has entered the market with an excellent machine and a rapidly growing user and software base. Hewlett-Packard has a long tradition in higher education and a sophisticated new entry into the microcomputer market. All four companies certainly merit consideration as part of a campus program. Table 6-2 compares the technical features of the four machine groups.

A COMMENT ABOUT THE OTHER BRANDS

What about the other 150 brands of microcomputers out there? Let us start this discussion by repeating our prejudice: *whenever possible stay mainline*. When you stick with the big mainline companies, you can rest assured that software will be written for the machines, service will be top-notch, and the innovations in future product lines will most likely be compatible with your equipment. You take an enormous risk if you buy a rela-

TABLE 6-2. COMPARING OUR FAVORITE MACHINES

Machine	Standard Processor	Memory Range	Standard Operating Systems	Standard Floppy Storage/2 Disks	Special Features
Apple MacIntosh	32 bit	128K	MAC	1 Drive 290K	Mouse, graphics
DEC Rainbow	Dual Processor 8 bit—Z-80 16 bit—8088	Standard: 64K Upgradable to: 986K	MS DOS CP/M	2 Drives 800K	High-resolution graphics, strong networking
IBM PC	16 bit—8088	Standard: 64K Upgradable to: 512K	PC DOS*	2 Drives 320-Single Density 640-Double Density	Much special software
HP150	16 bit 8088	Standard: 256K Upgradable to: 640K	MS DOS	2 Drives 528K	"Touch screen" operating procedure

*Same as MS DOS. CP/M available as extra cost option.
**CP/M available as extra cost option.

tively unknown brand. Stay out of the woods and on the main path. Those low-cost lures by the off-brands will inevitably turn out to have a hook in them.

A friend of ours argues, probably correctly, that it always pays to buy the very best you can afford. He calls this the "Mercedes Benz solution." The old saying reports that "you get what you pay for"; and modern experience verifies this. In the long run a Mercedes Benz is one of the most cost-effective cars on the road when you consider the resale value of the car. The same is true of the more expensive microcomputers. Generally, there is a direct relationship between the cost of the machine and what it will do. They may not cost less, but their cost-effectiveness ratio is excellent.

You may find that *specialized needs* sometimes dictate your choice. As we mentioned, both the Hewlett-Packard line of microcomputers and the DEC Professional 300 series are outstanding for heavy engineering programs. Moreover, both companies have a fairly large base of installed minicomputers on campuses throughout the nation. Consequently, some institutions might seriously want to consider the Hewlett-Packard line, the DEC Professional 300 series, or other specialized lines. The machines are often clear winners when juxtaposed against our set of criteria.

There is also the question of the "clones." A number of companies believe the way to succeed in the microcomputer field is to clone themselves after one of the Big Four. For example, the Franklin claims that it is totally compatible with the Apple II series—and the company claims to give you more for your money. There are at least a dozen companies claiming to have duplicated the IBM PC including compatibility with its software. What about these clones? Frankly, we are so convinced by our maxim to "stay mainline" that we have never seriously examined them. There are numerous magazine articles about them. An entire issue of *PC World* in April 1983 was dedicated to the IBM look-alikes. In general, we smell trouble with the clones. As *machines* they almost universally will cost less than the original machine they are imitating. This is their only claim to any consideration. But we worry about service, software compatibility, and long-term obsolescence. For example, much of the software written for the IBM machine will not simply plug in and successfully run on every clone. Several adaptations may be necessary. By and large, most campuses have plenty of problems deciding on appropriate software, appropriate computer literacy curriculum, and appropriate training programs. They do not need the extra headaches that often accompany non-mainline equipment. Of course, all this is subjective but we happen to think it's a pretty sensible prejudice! People have implemented successful campus programs with "off-brand" computers (that is, one not on our preferred list), but for every success story, we've heard three or four disaster scenarios.

THE SHAKEOUT IN THE MICROCOMPUTER INDUSTRY

We have been advocating throughout the book to "stay mainline," to stick with the major companies. Our advice stems partly from the apparent shakeout of the "smaller" computer companies. And, recently, the not-so-small have taken a tumble or two.

Unfortunately, some of the smaller firms may vanish from the industry without ever having sold one computer. Egil Juliussen of Future Computing, a marketing research firm, estimates that as many as two-thirds of the 150-plus microcomputer manufacturers have only "press-release products" (Rogers, 1983).

The following examples depict some problems in the industry:

Osborne

A company that went from nothing to $100 million in annual sales in only one and a half years filed for bankruptcy in late summer of 1983 and laid off 900 people.

Coleco Industries, Inc.

Delayed shipments of the company's new Adam Computer caused a major loss of the company's credibility in late 1983. In the midst of the shakeout, false promises will not benefit Coleco, as this is the company's first attempt to enter the home computer market.

Texas Instruments

In July and August 1983, sales were down—below planned levels. Second-quarter losses were approximately $183 million from home computer operations, and there was an estimated excess inventory of 150,000 units. In late October 1983 TI announced it was completely dropping its inexpensive home computer line, and many observers were worried about TI's commitment to its office-oriented, more expensive personal computers.

Franklin

This computer company was slapped with a lawsuit for imitating Apple Computer's operating system. Apple claimed copyright protection for its operating systems, which Franklin was blatantly using. The courts sided with Apple—and Franklin is in for a big dollar loss, and possibly a loss of customer confidence.

Atari

In a major shock to the home computer field, Atari laid off 3,000 workers, one-third of the staff, due to a loss of over $300 million in the second quarter of 1983. They misjudged the market for video games and suffered severely because of it.

Mattel

Mattel reported a loss of more than a half billion dollars for the first half of 1983. The loss resulted in layoffs of 37 percent of their electronics support staff and stock declines of 50 percent.

Victor Technologies

The company lost millions of dollars in 1983, laid off 950 people, and watched its stock drop from $22.25 to $5.75.

These stories are sad but true. The facts must be faced, and you, the decision maker, must be warned. Some people argue that the shakeout is not necessarily the end of the smaller computer companies. On the contrary, many new companies are entering the industry.

An article in the *Los Angeles Times* compares the present computer shakeout to the independent car dealers in the 1920s: "Independent car dealers came and went in those years; entrepreneurial computer makers like Adam Osborne come and go today" (Flanigan, 1983).

Actually, with any product you buy, the larger brands' companies in general are better able to back their products. When your television set or car breaks down, there is a company standing behind you to repair it. However, with computers you need the company to repair your computer but you also need to stay on top of the latest upgrading features and state-of-the-art developments in the computer world. This is all the more reason to stick with the larger companies.

There will inevitably be survivors all along the spectrum, from very successful to barely surviving. But regardless of who stays alive, it is definitely a safer bet to go with the mainline companies.

SUMMARY

Selecting the appropriate equipment is a critical feature for a successful campus-wide computer literacy program. In the previous chapters we have concentrated on selecting appropriate microcomputers. The first step is to obtain expertise and tap the brains of at least three different groups: inside experts, manufacturers, and consultants. The advice is the same for all three—listen carefully but take everything they say with a grain of salt. They may have built-in biases or positions to protect. Prejudices are obvious with the manufacturers, but they are just as important in consultants and your own home-grown experts.

The actual selection of equipment must be based on your unique campus needs. What kind of software will you be running? Should the campus support only one machine or is there sense in supporting several? In general, we lean in the direction of one machine for the whole campus, especially on small campuses. Anyone using a nonstandard machine can tell you a thousand reasons why multiple machines should be allowed. Usually, on a small campus the best advice is to plug your ears with cotton and push doggedly ahead with the single-machine notion. This move will insure compatibility of software, proper maintenance, and the spread of user expertise across the campus. Of course, large complex campuses may find that multiple brands may be needed for the unique concerns of various subunits.

What are the criteria for selecting the appropriate machine? First are the machine characteristics. It makes sense, whenever possible, to select equipment that has advanced along the evolutionary track. Second, a widespread use base is an extremely important factor. Which machine are other people using on your campus? What kind of software is readily available? What will be your specialized applications? What minicomputers are already being used and could serve in networks? In some cases, the user context issue may usually override the machine characteristics. For this reason, we think that some older machines such as the Apple IIe still deserve serious consideration. Software availability is a third criterion. In the field of education, software is not yet available from all vendors. Finally, cost is certainly a factor. Top-of-the-line machines will cost more, but it generally pays to stay mainline.

When we throw the machines on the market up against this set of criteria, we find only three companies—perhaps four if HP takes off—that produce truly mainline microcomputers. In spite of the relative antique status of the Apple II series, it nevertheless has a world of software and educational applications. It also has the largest user group of any machine and is less expensive than the other two companies. Moreover, Apple is introducing several new products including the Lisa and its less expensive little sibling MacIntosh. All these machines should be carefully examined. By contrast, IBM, DEC, and Hewlett-Packard have more expensive machines. However, the extra cost buys a much more sophisticated piece of equipment. IBM is clearly setting the sales pace at this point, with plenty of software being written for it. DEC is slow getting into the microcomputer market but is coming out with a superb line of machines. Since DEC has more minicomputers on campuses than anyone else, it may be the first company to offer superior "networking" capabilities. Hewlett-Packard shares some of DEC's advantages, because HP also has a large base of minicomputers on campuses.

There are over 150 brands of microcomputers on the market. Undoubtedly, quite a few of them are worthy of consideration. Until we can clearly see that the others have developed a significant user base and software supply, we will not be easily swayed by arguments on how good the equipment is. Undoubtedly, there is plenty of good equipment among the "off-brand" companies. However, without a solid user base, a breadth of user expertise, and a large software storehouse, we do not believe those machines are serious contenders for campuses. The decision is simply too important to stray off the mainline path and wind up lost in the woods.

The specific *brands* that fulfill our criteria will change rapidly, probably by the time this book is printed. But that is not the real point of this chapter. The *criteria* and *policy recommendations* outlined in Chapter 5 remain constant, and they are the real issue; the criteria and policies are the rocks of stability in the midst of a rapidly changing computer world.

CHAPTER 7

PRACTICAL ISSUES: ACCESS

TO MACHINES AND FINANCES

Earlier chapters discussed philosophical issues about starting a campus-wide computer competency program, about the debate between micro-computers and larger computers, and about selecting appropriate machines and software. This chapter deals with more mundane issues—financing, money, and purchase plans for faculty and students. Without successful solutions to these hard-nosed practical problems no campus computer program can succeed.

THE NATIONAL PICTURE: A BILLION A YEAR NEEDED

Robert Gillespie, vice-provost for computing at the University of Washington, conducted a study on computers in higher education (discussed in Magarrell, 1983e). His analysis indicated that colleges and universities would have to triple their present level of spending for equipment, programs, and staff in order to meet the computing needs of American college students. According to the President's Science Advisory Committee, an average of thirty hours per year of instructional computing per student would be required for undergraduate use. The computer resources now available allow each student less than ten hours of access per year. Consequently, the $300 million a year now being spent by colleges and universities for computers in instruction would have to be increased to $1 billion a year or more. This averages out to about $100 per student, which is roughly the amount now spent on libraries. Gillespie posits that "at least 20 to 40 hours per year will be required for the average undergraduate student—with more required for graduate programs and research" (Magarrell, 1983c). A *Chronicle of Higher Education* article went on to say:

> Richard L. Van Horn, provost of Carnegie-Mellon University, estimated
> that the capital investment for a "reasonable" computer system between

1985 and 1990 would be at least $1,000 per student at a liberal-arts college and up to $6,000 per student at a "high-technology school."

"At Carnegie-Mellon, with only 4,000 undergraduates and 1,500 graduate students," Mr. Van Horn said, "we expect to spend in excess of $20-million for equipment over the next five years."

Both Mr. Van Horn and Mr. Gillespie recommended that the federal government provide matching grants to encourage planning and financial commitment by colleges and universities—with help from industry and other sources—to make the capital investment required for adequate student access to computers.

They estimated it would take $200-million in matching funds to have a significant national impact on the problem.

Without such help, Mr. Van Horn said, "universities, regardless of their level of commitment, are unlikely to be able to generate all the capital required; even worse, they may not try."

Mr. Gillespie told the committee that such a program would follow the successful example of one administered by the National Science Foundation between 1956 and 1965. Federal matching grants totaling $70-million given to 184 institutions resulted in a total investment of more than $250-million in computers for instruction and research, he said.

". . . Leading-edge institutions, such as Carnegie-Mellon and Dartmouth, are now providing between 40 and 100 hours per student per year."

Mr. Gillespie said a program of federal matching grants should include incentives for industry to donate equipment or lend computer programs and personnel.

For example, he said, a university seeking to train engineering students in computer graphics might be able to borrow from the manufacturer expensive software that it couldn't afford to buy. Such loans could be encouraged by letting the university count them as matching funds and by offering the manufacturer a tax deduction for a charitable contribution, he said.

Carnegie-Mellon's Mr. Van Horn said that professional workers educated at "computer-intensive universities" had had a major influence on the use of computers in business and government in the past 30 years.

In the years ahead, he said, students educated at institutions with advanced systems of personal computers will spread the use of such systems as they move into professional jobs in the work force.

Mr. Van Horn said a second benefit to society from "computer-competent graduates" would be increased productivity in higher education as computers enhance learning and research.

Theodore Ricks, director of electronic publishing at Harper and Row Publishers, estimated that the average number of microcomputers per college has increased from six in 1980 to forty-five in 1983 and is expected to grow to 141 per campus in 1985 (Magarrell, 1983c, p. 9). The survey also estimated that 4 percent of all students and 10 percent of all faculty members in 1983 had access to a microcomputer at home or in their colleges. In short, much is happening on the national scene.

KEY OBJECTIVES FOR A LOCAL CAMPUS PROGRAM

Let us turn from the national to the local situation. In solving practical problems there are two key objectives: getting enough hardware and software into users' hands, and furnishing enough training so hardware is actually used. Thus, *access to machines* and *widespread training* are the key focal points.

Access to Machines

An institution simply cannot have an adequate computer training program without widespread access to computers. There is no way around this hard fact. Computer literacy and computer skills cannot be taught in the abstract; they cannot be obtained by listening to lectures. The only way to learn about computers is to use them and have a successful experience.

Computers should be provided in the normal place of work or study. The past history of computing is a centralized effort—the computer was placed in a central location and everyone came to it for service. The microcomputer revolution presses in the opposite direction—the computer comes to the users. As much as possible, campuses should make computing a decentralized opportunity available in the normal place where people work and study. Immediately, the average reader is likely to pose an important objection: "Isn't this totally idealistic considering the cost involved?" Certainly, a decentralized effort would be prohibitively expensive if we simply assumed the the institution was going to buy hundreds of microcomputers in one fell blow. But other financing arrangements (which we will discuss shortly) might soften the blow. The ideal is clear: users should have computers at their fingertips.

Purchase plans should allow faculty and students to own their own machines. There is an analogy between computing facilities and the library. Every campus maintains a central library that is a resource for the full community; by analogy every campus should have some computer laboratories for widespread community use. In addition to the library, most faculty and students buy many books on their own; people will purchase machines just as they purchase books. The difference, of course, is that machines cost substantially more than books. But the analogy is not far wrong if machines can be financed over time and the semester charges brought down to the $100 to $200 range.

Some central facility should be maintained as a general campus resource. The campus should not furnish *all* the microcomputers that everyone might need, but it should maintain *some* centralized services. At the very minimum the campus should maintain one or more microcomputer instructional laboratories. In addition, "drop-in" facilities are needed where people can practice. The campus need not supply the total demand for all students and faculty, because part of that burden will be borne by their own purchases. Nevertheless, many microcomputers should be maintained on the campus as a institution-wide resource—in laboratories, located in departmental offices, and at drop-in practice stations.

FINANCES

Financing a computer program is not cheap. However, an adequate program need not break the financial back of the campus. We suspect many policymakers have been scared off by the splashy newspaper announcements about IBM furnishing $25 million worth of equipment at Brown, or multi-millions being spent at Carnegie-Mellon, or $40 million given to MIT by DEC and IBM. Certainly a campus can embark on such a huge program, but the average college or university will mount substantially more modest programs. In fact, many small liberal arts colleges have put together computer competency programs, set up microcomputer laboratories, started employee purchase plans, and established training programs for under $100,000. Of course, the cost will depend on the campus's ambition.

Generating a "Multiplier Effect": More Byte for the Buck

How do we pay for a campus computer project? Most decision makers automatically assume the institution must foot the whole bill. Our experience suggests this is not necessarily so. Certainly the institution must be prepared to ante up significant funds to establish microcomputer laboratories and to mount a training program. But you should consider the *total* configuration of equipment and software around your campus, including the institution's resources and the resources of employees and students. It is possible to develop a fairly healthy body of equipment and software without the institution having to pay for it all. Basically there are four financing sources for a computer competency program:

1. institutional dollars
2. faculty, staff, and administrative private purchases
3. student private purchases
4. outside funds

On most successful campuses there is a complex mix of all four funding sources. Decision makers are often astonished at the willingness of faculty, staff, and students to purchase their own machines if the institution passes along the discounts it obtains from quantity purchases. Here is a key point: *a vigorous training program is the key to stirring up enthusiasm so that individuals will purchase their own microcomputers*. That is why the 50/25/25 rule is so critical. Rather than stretching your institutional funds to buy the last possible piece of equipment, develop a first-class training program that will stir up interest for personal purchases. Then consider those purchases part of the community resources. Given a choice, a little less equipment and a little more training will probably produce more equipment in the campus community. It is important to think about the *entire* resource base—both institutional and personal. Figure 7-1 is a graphic presentation of the cycle.

In short, we are emphasizing the need for a "multiplier effect." The institution should spend its dollars wisely so that each one produces a growth in expertise and enthusiasm that will help stir up the whole community to beat the financial burden for buying equipment. Later in this chapter we talk more about purchase plans for faculty, staff, and students.

Outside Funding: The "Local" Strategy

At every microcomputer conference someone always asks the $64 question: "Won't some computer company give us equipment, knowing that this is good advertising and that students will be captured by their brand?" Another variation of the question goes like this: "Can't we get a big foundation to make a splash by giving us a lot of money on this sexy issue?" Unfortunately, it is probably too late for both strategies. You

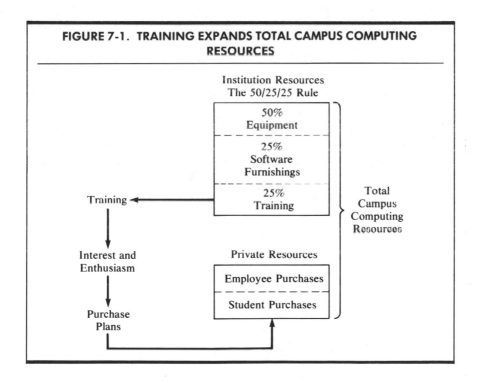

FIGURE 7-1. TRAINING EXPANDS TOTAL CAMPUS COMPUTING RESOURCES

FUNDING YOUR PERSONAL COMPUTER PURCHASES

If you are at a loss as to how you will possibly afford the computers for your campus, the following lists should be of some help.

If you go with one of the four computer companies we recommend, the following addresses and phone numbers should greatly assist you:

Apple Computer Corporation
Send postcard to:
Grants Information
Apple Education Foundation
20525 Mariani Avenue, Mail Stop 23-U
Cupertino, CA 95014
(408) 996-1010
Contact: Dr. Barbara Bowen

Digital Equipment Corporation
Corporate Contributions
Digital Equipment Corporation
111 Powder Mill Road
Maynard, MA 01754
(617) 493-2221
Contact: Nancy Dube

Hewlett-Packard Company
Corporate Contributions
Hewlett-Packard Company
P.O. Box 10301
Palo Alto, CA 94303-0891
(415) 857-1501
Contact: Emery Rogers

IBM Corporation
IBM Corporation
Old Orchard Road
Armonk, New York 10504
(914) 765-5165
Contact: Dr. Louis Robinson

If you decide on another line of computers, or simply need to know where else to look for grant money, the following is a list of some private foundations that might be able to help.

The Ford Foundation
320 East 43rd Street
New York, New York 10017

Charles Hayden Foundation
One Bankers Trust Plaza
130 Liberty Street
New York, New York 10006

The Martha Holden Jennings Foundation
700 National City Bank Building
Cleveland, Ohio 44113
(Limited to projects in Ohio)

Sid W. Richardson Foundation
2103 Fort Worth National Bank Building
Fort Worth, Texas 76102
(Limited to projects in Texas)

Alfred P. Sloan Foundation
630 Fifth Avenue
New York, New York 10111

The Spencer Foundation
875 North Michigan Avenue
Chicago, Illinois 60611

The John Jay and Eliza Jane Watson Foundation
507 Westminster Avenue
Elizabeth, New Jersey 07208

There are many other sources for funding. The following is a list of publications with current funding information.

Actionfacts
Published five times a year by the National Audio-Visual Association,
3150 Spring Street
Fairfax, Virginia 22031

Federal Grants and Contracts Weekly
Capitol Publications, Inc.
1300 N. 17th Street
Arlington, Virginia 22209

Chronicle of Higher Education
1333 New Hampshire Avenue, N.W.
Washington, DC 20036

*Classroom Computer News Directory of
Educational Computing Resources*
341 Mt. Auburn Street
Watertown, MA 02172

Computer Town Newsletter
ComputerTown, Box E
Menlo Park, CA 94025

Education Funding News
Education Funding Research Council
752 National Press Building, N.W.
Washington, DC 20045

could get the impression from reading *The Chronicle of Higher Educa-tion* that computer companies or foundations are throwing millions of dollars at this issue. That impression is not entirely wrong, because sub-stantial amounts of money were given to campuses from 1980 through 1983. But the publicity and advertising value to the computer companies and big foundations has now diminished sharply. Most have already made their big splash on this issue. There will, of course, be some computer issues that the big foundations and companies will fund, such as research on the *impact* of these programs and on their effectiveness in the curricu-lum. But for simply buying computers and setting up microcomputer laboratories the big national organizations have already spent their gener-osity. Of course, there will undoubtedly be a few more public announce-ments just to prove us wrong—but campus policymakers should not as-sume they will be the lucky ones!

However, the situation is not hopeless. Current opportunities proba-bly lie with *local* foundations, companies, and alumni. Many campuses have had good luck working with local foundations. Others have worked out excellent cooperative arrangements with local businesses who will swap equipment purchases for training. Major computer companies will still give substantial discounts even when they will not make outright gifts. And don't forget: a $50,000 microcomputer lab is just about the right size for a wealthy alumnus gift. Local resources, then, are likely to be the primary funders for basic equipment purchases. You will find other helpful funding information in the box on pp. 88-89.

ESTABLISHING INSTRUCTIONAL LABORATORIES

Campuses need microcomputer instructional laboratories. In the past, microcomputers were often placed in cubicles in the library or in a learn-ing assistance center. The whole concept of computers in cubicles was oriented toward individualized instruction. Although this strategy is not necessarily wrong it must be clearly supplemented by having instructional laboratories for classes. Training programs are important for both faculty, staff, and students, and any training program requires an instructional laboratory instead of computers facing a wall in cubicles. The laboratory should be equipped with twenty to thirty machines, with two disk drives each, with a common printer, and with significant audio-visual support. Large-screen monitors hooked up to the instructor's machine are needed so the entire class can observe it.

A classroom instructional laboratory will be invaluable as the campus mounts computer competency programs. But several logistical problems must be solved to make the lab work efficiently. *Scheduling* is a critical issue, of course. *Security* is another factor. Unfortunately, theft of microcomputers seems to be commonplace and every campus should take serious measures to protect them. In addition, *staff supervision* is essential. Many campuses use work-study students, supervised by a staff or faculty member. This is probably not a full-time job, and it can be an assignment along with a person's regular tasks.

Provisions must also be made for a *drop-in lab*. Students who have learned in a classroom will need considerable practice on the machine. The old style of having the computers in cubicles in the library works quite adequately for drop-in labs. The instructional laboratory can also be scheduled for drop-in use when no classes are scheduled. If you have to choose, setting up the instructional laboratory has first priority because it can serve as both a classroom and a drop-in lab. By contrast, computers in cubicles cannot serve effectively as a classroom. Of course, scheduling and supervision of the drop-in lab must be efficiently handled. Table 7-1 summarizes what is needed to set up a microcomputer lab.

The Cost of an Instructional Microcomputer Laboratory

The cost of a lab, of course, depends on what you put in it. Let us look at a configuration for a typical lab of twenty-four microcomputers. Here are our assumptions:

1. Each machine will have two disk drives.
2. A $3,000 software allowance will be included for the entire lab.
3. The lab will have substantial audio-visual equipment, but this will be obtained from the institution's existing inventory at no additional cost.
4. The lab will have one dot matrix printer.
5. Two additional large monitors will be attached to the instructor's computer so students can view them.
6. Furniture and extra large monitors can be obtained from the institution's existing inventory and will not present new expenditure.
7. No substantial renovation will be necessary in the physical space.

Given these assumptions Table 7-2 prices out three different laboratories, one using Apple IIe's, one using DEC Rainbows, and one using

---

TABLE 7-1. CHECKLIST FOR SETTING UP A MICRO-LAB

Equipment
Classroom role
Scheduling
Audio-visual aids
Software
Security
Staffing
Drop-in schedule

TABLE 7-2. PRICE COMPARISON ACROSS THREE COMPUTER BRANDS

Product Description	Number	Unit Retail	Retail Total	Discounted Educational Unit Cost	Total Educational Discount Cost
Apple Computers					
Apple IIe & DOS (64K)	24	1,395.00	33,480.00	1,046.25	25,110.00
Monitor	24	249.00	5,976.00	186.00	4,464.00
Disc IIe (with controller)	24	545.00	13,080.00	408.75	9,810.00
Disc IIe (w/o controller)	24	350.00	8,400.00	262.50	6,300.00
IIe Numeric Keypad	24	159.95	3,838.80	119.96	2,879.10
IIe 80 Column Card	24	125.00	3,000.00	93.75	2,250.00
IIe Stand	24	29.95	718.80	22.46	539.10
Dot Matrix Printer	1	695.00	695.00	521.25	521.25
Software Allowance	—		—		3,000.00

Retail Total: $72,188.60   Educational Discount Total: $54,873.45

Product Description	Number	Unit Retail	Retail Total	Discounted Educational Unit Cost	Total Educational Discount Cost
DEC Rainbows					
Rainbow System Unit (64K)	24	2,675.00	64,200.00	1,738.75	41,730.00
Black and White Monitor	24	325.00	7,800.00	211.25	5,070.00
Keyboard	24	245.00	5,880.00	159.25	3,822.00
CPM Operating System	24	250.00	6,000.00	162.50	3,900.00
Dot Matrix Printer	1	695.00	695.00	451.75	451.75
Software Allowance	—		—		3,000.00

Retail Total: $87,575.00   Educational Discount Total: $57,973.75

IBM PC

IBM, 2 double-sided disk drives					
w/keyboard (64K)	24	2,633.00	63,192.00	1,974.75	47,394.00
IBM Monichrome B/W Monitor	24	345.00	8,280.00	258.75	6210.00
Monitor Card	24	335.00	8,040.00	251.25	6,030.00
Dot Matrix Printer	1	695.00	695.00	521.25	521.25
Software Allowance	—		—	—	3,000.00

Retail Total: $83,207.00

Educational Discount Total: $63,155.25

Prices quoted in summer of 1983. These are not official discounts or prices. Contact your local dealer for current prices and discounts. In addition, we anticipate all these prices will fall in time—and with good negotiation!

IBM Personal Computers. In each case we have used prices that were current in late fall 1983, and have incorporated discounts commonly available at that time. The labs have similar configurations, including a ten-key numerical keypad, extremely useful for statistics and accounting.

In this example, then, the equipment costs are a little over $50,000 for all three machines (we suspect in some cases heavy bargaining could get the price down more). Using the 50/25/25 rule we arrive at a rough $100,000 total: $50,000 for machines; $25,000 for software, support, and physical space; and $25,000 for training. Of course, a single lab will not be sufficient when computing becomes commonplace, but the available equipment will be a good start when coupled with an attractive purchase plan.

Establishing a Software Library

How can software needs be handled? The campus should assemble a broad spectrum of software covering most programming languages, common office applications, computer-assisted instruction, and data management systems. These programs must be readily accessible for students, faculty, and staff. Remember, the machines are useless without an adequate software base. Here are some ideas.

The instructional lab can have a local area network with programs loaded on a hard disk. Most software companies sell hard disk versions of their programs, charging somewhat higher prices because they know multiple users will have access. For some situations the hard disk will be a good solution for the software problem. But you should examine this issue carefully because the hard disk and necessary networking equipment are relatively expensive—between $5,000 and $10,000 for a lab of twenty-four machines. You can buy a considerable amount of software for $10,000 so a careful investigation is important.

A check-out library with programs on floppy disks will be the most common solution. The software library must be near the machines, and an easy procedure for check-out must be established.

Large purchases of software can usually promote handsome discounts. In fact, 40 percent discounts are not uncommon for ten or more copies. Incidentally, it is usually easier to obtain discounts directly from the manufacturer or from a wholesale house, not from the local retail store.

A users' club can facilitate software sharing. Equipment manufacturers love users' clubs because they promote sales of their machines. By contrast, software vendors hate users' clubs because there is much copying and loaning of programs, thus cutting back on software sales. Copying software is sometimes illegal, depending on the software vendor's license agreements. However, some software vendors do not prohibit copying their software, and loaning software is rarely illegal. A good users' club can help substantially with software problems by spreading expertise, information, and evaluation of software. The best place to get good evaluation of software is from a user who knows it; one good place to find a knowledgeable person is in a users' club.

PURCHASE PLANS FOR FACULTY, STAFF, AND ADMINISTRATORS

The institution need not absorb the entire cost for a campus microcomputer resource base. A good training program can promote enough interest among campus employees to persuade a significant number to purchase their own computers.

Employee Purchase Plans

Many campuses have devised plans so employees can buy microcomputers at reduced prices. At the bare minimum campuses can pass along discounts obtained from quantity purchases. Discounts of 25 percent and 35 percent off the retail price are common. Usually this exceeds anything employees can get on their own.

In addition, many campuses offer a payroll deduction over a year or two to ease the purchase burden. *Chapman College,* for example, made arrangements to borrow money for microcomputer purchases, allowed the repayment to cover many months, and paid the interest as a subsidy for the program. Even if the interest charges were passed along to the employees the convenience of long-term payroll deductions would be attractive to many people.

Around the country many different schemes have been devised for helping faculty and staff purchase microcomputers. At *The University of Colorado,* for example, plans are being made to purchase more than 1,000 personal computers for faculty members (Turner, 1983). There is, however, a state law under which the university cannot sell computers to faculty members, but this may not be a barrier for the university. Faculty members will be able to use the personal computers under a user's fee arrangement. Chancellor Harrison Shull says that computers will be made available to faculty for a fee equal to one-third of the retail cost. Mr. Shull predicts the university's cost to be approximately $1.3 million. This decision will allow faculty members to do their own word processing and record-keeping, and to grow with the many other uses of the computer.

Western New England College has offered a payroll deduction plan for faculty and administrators to encourage the purchase of microcomputers. Through this program, the university purchases computers in mass quantity, thus receiving an 18 or 20 percent discount. Under an option-to-buy agreement, the computers are then leased to the employees and part of the purchase price is deducted from each paycheck for three years. After three years the employee may then buy the computer for one dollar.

Student Purchase Plans

Student purchase plans are very similar to employee plans. The minimal commitment by the institution ought to be to sell equipment to students at the discount rate over some period of time, with payments included in tuition and fee charges. Some colleges have placed microcomputers in dormitories and have added an extra charge on the dorm fee to amortize the equipment over a few years.

How large are the surcharges to the students to cover microcomputer cost? Of course, the answer depends on the type of computer bought, the discounts that were obtained, and whether students are sharing equipment (as they might well do in a dorm situation). In general, colleges have been charging about $200 a semester for the exclusive use of a microcomputer, and $100 for a shared machine. With generous discounts and a five-year amortization schedule these charges would cover a typical microcomputer, such as the three brands we have advocated.

Let's examine a few student purchase plans. At *Drexel University* in the fall of 1983 the freshman class (about 1,650 students) will be required to spend $1,000 for the new MacIntosh microcomputer by Apple (Magarrell, 1983f). The university will buy about 3,000 computers. Faculty members and upperclassmen will also have a chance to buy the computers. Drexel has an interesting philosophy in requiring students to purchase their own computers. They feel employers will look positively at students who could bring their own computers to work with them.

Another campus going computers, *Brown University,* proposes to provide a personal computer "work station" for each student and faculty member by 1989 (Magarrell, 1983e). Faculty and staff would be provided with computers on campus. If they desire additional home terminals, discounts would be made available. Students will be encouraged, not required, to buy their own personal computers. If the students decide to buy, they will receive some financial assistance from the university.

The program is estimated to cost $50 million to $70 million in its first five to seven years. William Shipp, associate provost for computing, sums up the reason for Brown University's proposed computer program. "We want to study the way scholars work—what they do and how they do it—and create a computing environment which lets them devise new ways to enrich and increase their work."

At *Clarkson College,* each freshman entering in the fall of 1983 will be furnished with a personal desktop computer (Magarrell, 1983e). The machine chosen for Clarkson students is the Zenith 1-100 desktop computer. The retail value of the computers exceeds $4,000, yet students will be charged only $200 per semester and a one-time maintenance fee of $200. When the students graduate after eight semesters, they may keep their computer, and will have paid only $1,800. Special grants by the college will help subsidize the machines' purchase.

It is predicted that by fall of 1986, networks will be developed so that every student at Clarkson will have access to the other students' machines, to professors' machines, as well as to the college's main computer.

Stevens' Institute of Technology has been involved with microcomputers for sometime (McDonald, 1982). In 1982, Stevens's freshmen entering the sciences, the systems planning, and the management areas were required to buy the Atari 800 personal computer. Freshmen entering the engineering field, however, were not required to buy their own—instead, they used the institute's central computer facilities.

In 1983, Stevens's students entering all three areas of engineering science were required to buy a personal computer. Edward A. Friedman, dean of the college, feels that today's requirement to buy a microcomputer is similar to the old requirement when engineering students had to buy a certain kind of slide rule. Stevens's computers from 1983 forward will be the Digital Equipment Company's Professional 325 and will cost the student $1,800 as compared to $750 for the Atari 800. The DEC personal computer has sixteen times as much internal memory, dual disk drives, and is more sophisticated than the Atari. When the students graduate, they may either keep the equipment or sell it—just like a textbook.

Dean Friedman feels that having the students own their computers rather than leasing or borrowing them from the institute would make the students "identify with the computer and begin to think of it as a permanent part of their intellectual system."

Purchase Plans for Students and Faculty: The Need for One Machine

Earlier in the book we argued that there ought to be a campus policy to support a single machine. This carries over into the purchase programs. It is foolish for the campus to make a policy about having one machine under institutional purchases, and then allow proliferation under the individual purchases that it sponsors. Certainly no one can tell individual purchasers what they have to buy; on the other hand, the campus does not have to help underwrite purchases that proliferate brands. This is clearly true if the college is subsidizing the purchases, but also if the campus is only passing along quantity discounts. Why would an institution be making quantity purchases of nonstandard machines? Not just so individuals can buy nonstandard machines that cause more headaches! Remember, the reason the campus is supporting individual purchases is to help establish a *total community resource*. If people insist on buying nonstandard machines they really are not contributing to that community resource, so there is no reason why the campus should support their purchase. The logic seems consistent: one machine, even if it makes some people mad.

CHAPTER 8
STAFF TRAINING
PROGRAMS

Faculty and staff training is mandatory. Training is a key for building faculty and staff enthusiasm, for integrating the microcomputers into the cirriculum, for generating employee interest in purchasing their own microcomputers, and for building fundamental expertise that will permeate the campus. Unfortunately there is a strong temptation for campuses to spend all of their money on *hardware,* neglecting the *human issues* of training. Usually campus administrators are eager to stretch their scarce resources as far as possible and purchase as many machines as feasible. This frequently produces two disasters: the purchase of inexpensive machines that are quickly outgrown, and neglect of the training that is the fundamental base of the enterprise. We subscribe strongly to our self-invented 50/25/25 rule. Fifty percent of your available money should be allocated to your equipment; 25 percent to software, supplies, audio-visual support, and furnishings; and 25 percent to a faculty/staff/administrator training program. It is a serious mistake to spend all of your money on equipment without attention to the software and training efforts that make the equipment useful!

FACULTY AND STAFF TRAINING PROGRAMS

When colleges have simply dumped machines on the campus without any plan for staff training the results have been mixed. In some cases the program took off because of the interest and effort of a few people. This is particularly true on campuses with heavy scientific and engineering backgrounds where people were already accustomed to mainframe computer usage. But in other cases the machines sat virtually idle, locked away in some lab and only sparsely used. Rarely does a campus realize the full potential of its program without a systematic effort to train faculty, staff, and administrators.

The Weakness of Self-Teaching

How do people learn to use microcomputers? Certainly one big advantage of microcomputers is the "user-friendly" software that can be learned by anyone who is willing to dedicate the time and energy. In fact, the vast majority of people have learned their user skills by reading the manual and by hard practice. Why not simply let everyone teach themselves? Why pay for a training program?

The manuals are often difficult to use. The software manuals vary considerably—from bad to terrible! Unfortunately, documentation and instructions have lagged far behind the quality of the software itself. Almost everyone finds the manuals obtuse. The learning curve, shown in Figure 8-1 is flat for quite a while. That is, learning is slow. Then after considerable practice and work with the manuals the learning curve finally takes off rapidly. But until the learner reaches the takeoff point continual frustration can be a problem.

Individual learning leads to uneven skills across the campus. When each person learns alone, there is little in common to the learning pattern. This is a problem when staff need to work on office activities together, or when faculty try to implement curriculum changes together, or when administrators want to exchange data bases and files.

Individual learning causes proliferation of software types. When everybody does their own training each person will be picking software. Proliferation of, say, five word processing programs on a campus leads to chaos—files will not transfer and skills are not usable across programs. A proliferation of software for the same purpose has all the drawbacks of

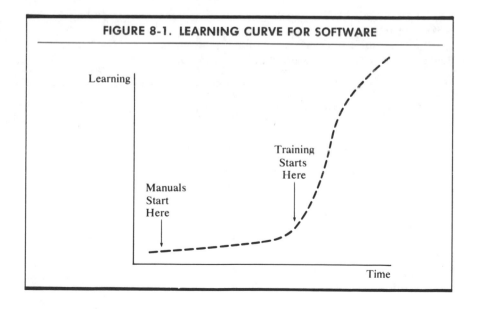

FIGURE 8-1. LEARNING CURVE FOR SOFTWARE

machine proliferation that we identified in Chapter 4. The disadvantages of individual learning are summarized in Table 8-1.

Advantages of a Training Program

A campus training program offers many advantages.

1. *Training provides more uniform skills across the campus, and provides more software compatibility.* An adequate training effort ensures that everyone learns the same software. For example, everyone's word processing files can be exchanged. When the secretary is sick the replacement will know the same word processing software; when the English faculty teaches composition the word processing package will be common; when students steal each other's term papers the uniform files won't mess them up!

2. *Training generates group enthusiasm.* When a group of faculty, staff, and administrators go through training together a sense of excitement is usually generated. A mutual support group emerges, short-circuiting much of the lonely frustration of a manual-reading single learner.

3. *Training significantly speeds the learning process.* Look again at Figure 8-1. Training hurries everyone through the flat part of the learning curve, quickly moving the group into the more gratifying success curve. The benefits are triple: quicker learning, more success, less frustration.

4. *Training permits more in-depth coverage.* When people are learning individually they have enough on their hands just learning baseline skills. They hardly have the time, the expertise, or the experience to branch out into specialized areas. A good training program, using experienced teachers, can provide more specialized information. For example, a training instructor who is an expert on computer-assisted instruction will have years of experience to share. In this field like any other, a skilled teacher brings a wealth of background that can be shared with the learners in a fraction of the time they could dig the information out for themselves. Table 8-2 summarizes the advantages of a training effort.

Inside or Outside Trainers?

In Chapter 4 we said *inside* experts had some advantages (intimate knowledge of the campus, familiarity with local people, curriculum, and

---

TABLE 8-1. DISADVANTAGES OF INDIVIDUAL SELF-TEACHING

Slow
Uneven learning
Manuals terrible
Proliferation of software
Less likely to pick good software

TABLE 8-2. ADVANTAGES OF TRAINING PROGRAMS
Speeds learning Builds group enthusiasm Gives wider exposure to software Provides uniform software base

needs) and some disadvantages (lack of time, other commitments, personal axes to grind). *Outsiders* also have strengths (expert knowledge, lack of entanglement with local politics, and fewer turf questions to fight for) as well as weaknesses (ignorance of local conditions). In the training arena the same insider/outsider advantages exist.

Most campuses may have enough experts to mount an in-house training effort, but there are problems. At first blush in-house experts will seem cheaper than outside trainers. But that simple assumption may be questionable when closely examined. A good training program requires at least three things: *expert knowledge* about microcomputers (probably available on campus); *time* to prepare a training curriculum and *experience* running this type of activity (items probably *not* readily available). In short, your local experts will know about micros but probably will not have the time, the freedom from other obligations, and the specific training experience to quickly mount a serious program.

Outside training groups bring several advantages:

1. they can mount a training activity quickly, since they will have the curriculum ready;
2. they can bring a wealth of experience from other training programs;
3. they can bring broader background on specialized subjects (such as computer-assisted instruction);
4. fees can often be lower than equivalent released time for faculty and other costs.

A combination insiders/outsiders is often effective. A good combination on training is to bring in an outside training group for a basic, quick-starting series of workshops. At the same time a "training corps" of half a dozen local people are designated to work with the outsiders and to continue training efforts after the consultants leave. This combination gives the advantages of both insiders and outsiders:

- ∘ quick start-up (outside strength)
- ∘ well-prepared, experienced training program (outside strength)
- ∘ broad experience, specialized knowledge (both)
- ∘ followthrough in the local setting (inside strength).

Table 8-3 summarizes the advantages of outside trainers.

TABLE 8-3. ADVANTAGES OF OUTSIDE TRAINERS

Quick start-up
Prepared curriculum
Broader special skills
Experience running this exact program
Cost effective

Who Should Get Training?

According to a recent survey, 82 percent of faculty want to take instructionally oriented computer courses, yet less than 20 percent have received training thus far (Reed, 1982). More than twenty new bills to help underwrite teacher training efforts have come before Congress in the last few years. This reflects the growing realization that administrative and faculty training are essential to the success of any campus-wide computer competency program. Some of these bills, designed to encourage training programs, would provide increased tax deductions for businesses that contribute computer facilities to colleges and universities. For instance, in 1983 IBM donated fifteen IBM personal computers to seven teacher-training institutes in California, Florida, and New York. Professors at the colleges will attend a two-week seminar to learn to teach computer literacy.

The Tandy Corporation, owner of Radio Shack, is also contributing to training efforts by mailing instructional handbooks and basic computer-literacy packages to 103,500 schools in the United States. In addition, it is offering teachers free programming classes on Radio Shack equipment. According to Richard Van Horn, provost of Carnegie-Mellon University, without the cooperation from industry and other sources, "universities, regardless of their level of commitment, are unlikely to be able to generate all the capital required for adequate student access to computers; even worse, they may not try."

Who should be trained in such a program? We think it is highly desirable to have *all* of the college personnel exposed to some microcomputer training. Yes, this means faculty members, secretaries, maintenance people, administrators, and even the presidents and vice-presidents! Top administrators who learn to use microcomputers are strong advocates of the program; faculty members who master microcomputers will reshape their courses and benefit the students; secretaries who can use a microcomputer are invaluable as support people. Needless to say, every campus will set up its program differently and may have different priorities for who learns. But we feel that expanded access and training is essential across the entire campus.

What should the training programs contain? They should have a healthy dose of both "knowledge about" and "work on." "Knowledge about" means information about how computers work and the theory of computing. "Work on" means hands-on experience and mastery of several software pieces.

"Knowledge About" Computers

A training program should explore general issues about computers. The topic list could be extremely long, but here is the bare minimum:

1. *How Computers Work.* Participants should be given an overview in nontechnical language about how the computer functions, including memory processes, input devices, and output devices. The material in Chapter 2 of this book is roughly what we mean.

2. *Computer sizes, types, and functions.* Participants need to know the difference between mainframe, minis, and microcomputers. A list of advantages and disadvantages of the three types would also be useful. Chapter 2 has this kind of information.

3. *The range of software.* Most people do not know the extensive computer software base that exists, and it would be very helpful to give people a sense of what computers will do for them.

4. *Criteria for selecting equipment.* In Chapter 4 we outlined criteria for selecting equipment. Participants in campus training should clearly understand these criteria, or another set you believe is more appropriate. In any event they need guidance about how to select and buy equipment because many will be making purchases.

5. *Knowledge about specific software packages.* Participants should also be given specific information about software in five or six common fields. The training program ought to offer criteria for selecting software just as it does for equipment.

6. *Literature for more information.* The training programs should refer participants to literature, including books and magazines, where they can get more information.

"Work On" Computers

Talking about computers is a good starting point but there is no substitute for hands-on experience. Computer Horizons Project at UCLA has done scores of workshops for faculty and administrator training. Interestingly enough, we have often been invited simply to give a "talk" workshop. We always refuse. We have a rigid requirement that at least half of any workshop is devoted to hands-on experience with the computer. There is simply no substitute for this personal interaction with the machine, even in the most elementary training activity. What kinds of hands-on experience should be included in a training program? A baseline for any computer training program should include mastery in five software groups: utilities, word processing, graphics, budget spread sheets, and data base management systems.

THE COMPUTER HORIZONS PROJECT AT THE GRADUATE SCHOOL OF EDUCATION, UCLA

The Computer Horizons Project is a program of the Higher Education Research Institute in the Graduate School of Education at UCLA. Partly funded by Digital Equipment Corporation, the program was established to provide training and consultation to educators trying to implement campus-wide computer programs. The program, directed by J. Victor Baldridge, also evaluates, develops, and disseminates quality microcomputer programs to colleges and universities throughout the nation. The specific services provided by the program are as follows:

1. Installation of Campus-Wide Microcomputer Programs

Through a series of nationwide workshops and on-site consulting efforts, Computer Horizons works with campuses who want to develop campus-wide installation efforts. Included are topics such as hardware and software selection, policy development, faculty training, administrative systems and software, access to computers, purchase plans for faculty and students, curriculum adaptation, and linkage issues.

2. Training

Computer Horizons has established a microcomputer teaching lab at UCLA for training.

- *A Basic Introduction* to the machine covers hardware knowledge and terminology, general uses of a computer and utilities.
- *Administrative/Professional* computer use is a succession of workshops geared for success with prepackaged applications software such as word processing, electronic spreadsheets, data base management, and graphics.
- *Computer Assisted Instruction:* how it works, how to select and evaluate it, and where to find it are the topics of this workshop.

3. "Trainer of Trainers" Activities

The Computer Horizons workshops utilize a "trainer of trainers" model so various institutions can implement their own efforts when returning to their campus. On-site campus training can also be arranged.

---

1. *Utilities.* The Training programs should teach the various basic nuts and bolts activities incorporated into the "utilities" operating system. The utilities include such mundane activities as copying a disk, formatting a disk, configuring the machine to use various accessories, and setting up file structures. Without some acquaintance with these routine procedures the user is completely lost.

2. *Word Processing.* Word processing will be the number one use of computers on most campuses, so an extensive set of lessons is mandatory. These lessons should include some fairly sophisticated uses such as mail merge, variables, block moves, search and change operations, and dictionary functions.

3. *Simple Graphics.* Graphics can enrich publications, lectures, and presentations. They can be invaluable for spicing up the college classroom. And most people enjoy the fun of creating a bar chart, whipping up a pie chart, and drawing out a line graph. Add some color graphics and you have a recipe for an enjoyable activity that most people can readily learn.

4. *Budget Spreadsheets.* Budget spreadsheets like Visicalc or Multiplan are extremely popular, and there is a darn good reason: they are amazingly powerful budgeting tools with an enormous range of practical applications. Almost everyone can find a good use for these powerful programs; many people get "hooked" on computers because they find spread sheets so down-to-earth practical.

5. *Data Base Management System.* Electronic filing systems with built-in "report generators" are an important use of computers. Mastering some simple data base management system is essential.

A valid training program should include honest *mastery* of these five software packages. This should not be an introductory smattering of superficial work. When people leave the training program they should be able to use these five programs. Ample opportunity should also be afforded for practice, the essential ingredient that spells success.

Programming?

What about the perennial question: "Should programming languages be included in the personnel training program?" We will argue this issue vis-à-vis the student curriculum in Chapter 7, and our position is the same for the faculty, staff, and administration. There is probably no reason for most college personnel to study programming, particularly administrators and staff who want to solve practical problems with the computer. A few faculty members in specialized areas will of course wish to learn programming. But in general training programs for college personnel we doubt that programming is essential. In fact, since programming is likely to frighten, bore, and turn off some people we definitely think it should *not* be required as part of a general training program for your personnel. Only people who really need it and really want it should be provided the opportunity to learn it.

A TRAINING PROGRAM IN ACTION: CHAPMAN COLLEGE

At Chapman College in Orange, California, a computer literacy training program has been in effect since April 1983. Chapman College is a liberal arts college with bachelor's programs in thirty-eight areas including com-

A SAMPLER OF TRAINING ACTIVITIES FOR FACULTY AND STAFF
(WHO'S DOING WHAT)

The National Institute for Retraining in Computer Science
Potsdam, New York
> The retraining program will be conducted at Clarkson College in 1983 and 1984. It will consist of two eight-week summer sessions with additional work during the following academic year. The main goal here is to prepare faculty members from other fields to teach computer related courses.

Radio Shack Computer Centers
600 centers throughout U. S.
> Free instruction is available to all college and university teachers by simply presenting a letter from their institution to waive the class fees. Instruction covers an introduction to TRS 80 computers, programming in BASIC, and computer usage in the classroom. Classes meet in the evenings and on weekends.

St. Lawrence University
Canton, New York
> Faculty members here are being offered a stipend to attend free computer workshops. This $250.00 incentive was available to any faculty member taking a computing course in the summer of 1983. The effort was to encourage faculty members from different departments to use the campus computer system in their teaching and research. The stipend money comes from a separate "dean's faculty-development fund."

College of Notre Dame
Belmont, California
> CND offers its faculty and staff over a dozen microcomputer training workshops. The college has a DEC Rainbow microcomputer lab where the workshops are held.

Chapman College
Orange, California
> Chapman implemented a computer literacy training program in April 1983. Forty Apple IIe computers and accessories were installed to complete the training lab. Workshops are free of charge to faculty, staff, and administrators.

Lambuth College
Jackson, Tennessee
> Using Title III federal funds, Lambuth has offered its staff and faculty members a series of microcomputer training workshops. The workshops included a general introduction to microcomputers, and hands-on training in data base management, word processing, graphics and electronic spreadsheets. Software and campus policy issues were also covered.

Teacher Training Institutes
> IBM is donating PC's to seven universities in California, Florida, and New York. Professors at these colleges will attend a two-week seminar on computer literacy.

Computer Horizons
Graduate School of Education, UCLA
> A series of miniconferences through the 1983-84 and 1984-85 academic years is being sponsored all across the United States for campus policymakers. The Digital Computer Company funded the program, which is expected to cover hundreds of administrators and trustees in two-day policy conferences. Hands-on training will be part of the effort.

puter science, graduate degrees offered in sixteen fields, and credential programs for teachers and specialists in nine areas. There are 1,100 students from thirty-nine states and thirty-five foreign countries. There are 100 full-time faculty members teaching classes with an average of only twenty students. Chapman also has over forty Residential Educational Centers around Southern California. These are basically outreach efforts that take educational programs to decentralized locations.

Eager to begin the computer literacy program at Chapman, President G. T. Smith gave his approval for planning to get underway in January 1983. Hans Jenny, vice-president for financial affairs, and Cameron Sinclair, vice-president for academic affairs, took the lead in developing details of the program. As a result of the planning, a complete microcomputer training lab was set up on campus. The lab houses forty Apple IIe microcomputers, each with disk drives and monitor. There are large TV monitors in the lab to enable the students to see as well as hear what is going on. These audio-visual aids are a definite asset to the learning process.

Training began in the spring of 1983. The first computer literacy "students" were Chapman faculty, staff, and administrators. The idea was to train the faculty, and they in turn would train their students. The authors of this book set up the training program. Training primarily involved teaching faculty, staff, and administrators to use computers in their own professional capacity. Dozens of hands-on workshops were held in the areas of:

1. an overview of computer literacy including an introduction to the microcomputer
2. utilities
3. graphics
4. budget spreadsheets
5. word processing

6. data management
7. statistics

As a result of the training workshops, interest levels in microcomputers grew rapidly. A purchase plan was developed to enable faculty, staff, and administrators to take personal computers into their homes. The college loaned faculty members money to purchase the computers, and the loan was to be paid back over a year. Substantial discounts from Apple were also offered to make the computers more affordable. Over 100 faculty and staff used the purchase plan to obtain computers.

In addition to faculty training, students were inaugurated into the computer literacy program in the fall of 1983. Dr. Cameron Sinclair, vice-president for academic affairs, told us what Chapman was trying to achieve for its students:

> Our main goal is to have every Chapman student familiar with computers, to be comfortable with the machines. The English department is taking the lead, introducing the program with word processing in the English composition classes. Every freshman has to enroll in English Composition, so word processing will be the main software application involved. However, other selected software will be added to the classroom situation to familiarize the students with available programs. By then adding some programming every student will have the opportunity to become a competent microcomputer user.

Another aspect of the computer literacy program, according to Dr. Sinclair, is that each major will be encouraged to incorporate computer activities in whatever manner is appropriate to that particular discipline. Each major will teach software applications pertaining to the major as well as certain selected software outside the major. The point is to offer a broadened view to the students. Within each major two or three courses will allow hands-on computer time. The ultimate goal is to help students become knowledgeable about microcomputers *and* to apply their knowledge successfully to disciplinary tasks.

In sum, Chapman's main objectives for the student computer literacy program are:

1. to help students overcome computer anxiety by exposing them to microcomputers in their mandatory Freshman English Composition classes;
2. to introduce the microcomputer as it is relevant to each major. Hands-on experience will be a large part of the coursework. Also, the curriculum will include some software applications *other* than the major;
3. to give students some understanding of computers—what they can and cannot do. And, of course, the students will be able to use them successfully.

The college has not yet started a purchase plan for students. Dr. Sinclair says the most desirable plan would be to put a computer in each dorm room. With a small increase in dorm fees, students would pay off the computer in four years. Thus, the students would own the machine by the time they graduate.

Dr. Sinclair feels that unsuccessful students do not achieve in college due to a lack of motivation and interest. Somewhere along their education career they have been turned off. He hopes that through the computer literacy program the students' motivation levels will increase. In fact, a pilot program was instigated in the summer of 1983 in order to enhance the success of borderline academic students. Incoming freshmen admitted provisionally took a seven-week intensive summer program in mathematics, analytical reading, and composition. Microcomputers were introduced in the math and composition courses. The college hoped that the new technology would help motivate the students to learn. This was indeed the case. The program was designed to break through the psychological "lack-of-interest" barrier these students had built up over the years. The program has proven to be quite successful.

Most of the larger computer literacy programs have taken place in the "high tech" institutions such as Carnegie-Mellon, Stevens Institute of Technology, and the California Institute of Technology. On these campuses, computer science and engineering are the main thrust of the curriculum. Chapman, a liberal arts college, has also successfully entered the campus computer literacy movement that is sweeping the nation.

COMPUTER USERS' GROUPS

The "formal" training efforts outlined above can be enormously supplemented through the "informal" training offered by users' groups. Users' groups have popped up at campuses all across the country. There are frequent notices in the student newspaper for meetings of the Apple Club, Osborne Group, Rainbow Users, and other clubs. Users' clubs are an important way to spread expertise about computers and information about software, equipment, and ways of solving common problems. Let us look at one campus that has a thriving computer competency program, with a massive users' club as a foundation. That campus is California State University at Long Beach (CSULB).

CSULB is a state university with an enrollment of 30,000. Microcomputers have been popular on campus for several years. Most of the popularity is due to the Learning Assistance Center which has been promoting the use of the Osborne personal computer. The portable Osborne microcomputer runs CP/M software, thus opening up a wide variety of software options.

"OPEN" (Osborne Professionals and Educators Network) is a users' group that was founded in March 1983 at CSULB by Frank Christ. The purpose of the users' group as stated in the "OPEN" bulletin is:

> ... to bring together college and university faculty, students, staff, and members of the surrounding community who own or use ... or who want to explore owning or using Osborne computers or other CP/M machines like the Kaypro, Otrona, Xerox 820.
>
> The emphasis in "OPEN" is on the college and university community and its needs with member activities and benefits focusing on the following objectives:
>
> 1. Increasing Microcomputer literacy.
> 2. Learning about and using applications software.
> 3. Developing and using CAI (Computer-aided-instruction).
> 4. Sharing ideas and software with colleagues.

Some membership services offered are:

> Monthly meetings
> Weekend workshops
> Discounts on hardware and software
> Access to public domain software
> Access to software exchange library
> Microcomputer materials library
> Newsletter (10 issues yearly)

Having been in existence for only five months, "OPEN" has 130 active members. Users' groups are an extremely effective way to broaden one's knowledge in the computing world.

*   *   *   *   *

Training programs, purchase plans, users' clubs, and laboratories for practice are all elements in a faculty and staff development effort. Such an effort is at the heart of a campus-wide program, a necessary first step before curriculum innovation can occur—a subject that comes up in the next chapter.

CHAPTER 9

CURRICULUM ISSUES:

CONNECTING THE COMPUTERS

AND THE CURRICULUM

All this talk about buying computers, setting up microcomputer laboratories, and developing training programs has one fundamental objective: to get the computers into the hands of students in the classroom. This chapter examines the ways in which computers can be spread across the campus.

First, we will look at how computers are currently used in the curriculum. Second, we will examine the debate regarding programming languages. Third, we will suggest how colleges can make rapid progress in curriculum adaptation without huge expense and without endless programming problems. Finally, we will examine some common "canned" computer-assisted instruction (CAI) packages that can simply be purchased.

SIGN OF THE TIMES: THE EXPLOSION OF COMPUTER TEXTBOOKS

Formal textbooks in the fields of computers began to appear only twenty years ago; today they number in the thousands (Winkler, 1982).

A few facts about computer textbooks:

- Prentice-Hall, computer sciences' largest publisher, lists about 1,000 computer-related text and reference books.
- Addison-Wesley Publishing Company has moved from computer books comprising 0.5 percent of its sales in 1974 to over 15 percent in 1982.
- There are over 3,000 computer related science texts available to college students, according to Doris Lidtke, a professor of computer science at Townson State College, who compiles an annual list of

111

such books for libraries. This figure includes only computer science course books and not those in other areas of computer applications.

The Growth of Computer Related Courses

Until the last few years, computer science was not a large area for textbooks. Suddenly, with the introduction of the term "computer library" there has been an explosion of books. Daniel Cougar, who edits *The Computing Newsletter* for business schools which runs an annual list of computer-science textbooks, sees the market growing just as large as any other introductory subject required of all students, such as English.

Twenty-five years ago, there were almost no computer books, says Karl Karlstrom, a computer science editor at Prentice-Hall. In 1960 only several dozen books on the subject were available, and for the most part these were computer language books. In 1968, the first nonlanguage computer book was published by Addison-Wesley. And in 1970 a whole series of books began to emerge in many areas, such as using computers to solve nonmathematical problems. Another spurt came in 1975; now everyone is trying to get into the area. Mr. Cougar of the *Computing Newsletter* estimates that there are about 175 publishers competing in the computer science market today.

A TAXONOMY OF COMPUTER USE IN THE COLLEGE CURRICULUM

Hans Jenny, vice-president of Chapman College, has devised a very useful taxonomy of computer use in the college curriculum. His basic classification is shown in Table 9-1.

Traditional Uses of Computers

Computing has been a significant factor in the college curriculum for about twenty years. Computers were used for (1) teaching computer science, (2) special program applications, (3) packaged scientific applications, and (4) simple programming languages. Probably the bulk of the computing time was used for programming and for scientific applications. (We are strictly talking here about academic applications, not the more common administrative activities.)

However, the coverage of the student body was extremely thin, with probably no more than 5 to 10 percent of the average student body having any significant contact with computers. In fact, this is probably an accurate description of today's situation.

Computer-Assisted Instruction

Computer-assisted instruction (item 5 of Table 9-1) is the use of the computer to teach a whole course, or to supplement the course with in-

TABLE 9-1. COMPUTER USAGE IN THE COLLEGE CURRICULUM	
1. Computer science	The development of computer theory, technology, and software. Interaction with mathematical science to extend computer sciences.
2. Special program applications	High-level, especially programmed computer applications for major physical sciences and mathematics applications.
3. Packaged scientific applications	Natural and social science research application using "pre-packaged software" (e.g., SPSS or SAS for social science).
4. Simple programming languages	Nontechnical programming in languages (e.g., BASIC, COBOL, PASCAL).
5. Computer-assisted instruction	Packaged programs that actually teach an entire course of instruction (e.g., Plato or the counseling series called SIGI).
6. Adaptation of general software	User-oriented packaged programs requiring no knowledge of programming (e.g., word processing, accounting software, data base management).

NOTE: The basic ideas for this chart were developed by Hans Jenny, executive vice-president of Chapman College.

struction on the computer. Typically an entire curriculum is constructed and taught at the keyboard of the computer. Over twenty years of effort were directed toward computer-assisted instruction, but these efforts were hamstrung by excessive costs, by reliance on expensive mainframes, and by faculty resistance. Probably fewer than 1 percent of American college students have ever experienced computer-assisted instruction.

Adaptations of General Software

Item 6 of Table 9-1, packaged general applications, consists of software such as word processing, statistics, data base management systems, and business packages. Few prepackaged programs were widely used in the curriculum up to now. They were very expensive, usually available only on mainframes, and the microcomputer versions have only recently emerged. Nevertheless, we suspect that preprogrammed packages will be a major future trend in the curriculum.

Look again at Table 9-1. Items 1–4 have been the staple commodities of computer usage, but they have covered only about 5 to 10 percent of the students. In the future we think items 4–6 will be the new staple commodities, and they will then be covering probably 90 percent of the students! The other functions will not go away, but the mass appeal of computer-assisted instruction and preprogrammed packages will promote their widespread use.

Here is our prognosis. The history of college computing has moved *down* Jenny's chart, beginning with computer science. The big breakthroughs of the immediate future will move *up* the chart, by using preprogrammed software adapted to the college curriculum, by using computer-assisted instruction administered with micros, and by introducing programming more widely. The next few sections examine some issues in these trends.

THE BIG DEBATE: PROGRAMMING VERSUS APPLICATION SOFTWARE

For the last twenty years the motto has been clear: "The computer is king." When people wanted to talk to computers they talked in the machine's language—programming languages. Because the machines were scarce and extremely expensive it was easier to *adapt the people to the machines*. If you wanted to talk to a computer you learned how to program, it was that simple.

In recent years computers have become commonplace and the human–machine interaction is no longer rare. The revolution in software has a new motto: "The human is king." The microcomputer *adapts the machine to the people*. The new user-friendly softwares are a revolution in people–machine interface. Now most people who use computers will never learn to program, they will be proficient in preprogrammed software.

What is the implication for the curriculum? Will we continue to teach programming or will the new software packages eliminate that need? Some people will insist that programming is mandatory. The New Converts, who got involved with computers because of user-friendly software, will say that prepackaged software should be the backbone of a computer competency program.

In some ways this is a tempest in a teapot. For the heavy computer users in math, science, and computer science, programming will continue to be a critical skill. But prepackaged software applications will probably be the backbone of a broad computer effort in the general education curriculum. Student enthusiasm will be ignited for tackling real-world problems, such as using a word processor for English Composition. The issue is not programming *versus* applications software. Rather, we will have healthy doses of both, with sharp variations depending on the users and their needs.

We agree that programming will continue to be important, but we still insist that there is a high payoff in prepackaged software. It allows the student to solve real-world problems immediately, generating excitement without the tedium of programming. Some people may argue that without programming the student is having a "superficial" encounter with the computer. Perhaps so, but the encounter is better than being scared off by programming! Our philosophy is simple: hook the students with interesting prepackaged programs and they will love computing. Then we can help them grow with additional programming languages.

Kenneth C. Green, a researcher at UCLA, stated the distinction between the two approaches well. He noted in a recent speech that programming was an "indirect" method of solving problems. As opposed to this *programmer-smart* approach, Green suggests that the preprogrammed software helps students be *problem-savvy*. The problem-savvy approach allows students to move rapidly into a feeling of mastery and accomplishment.

In any event, we suspect this common debate in today's discussions will seem like an antique in a few years. Soon we will undoubtedly have widespread computer competency with rich mixes of both programming and prepackaged software.

CURRICULUM ADAPTATION OF EXISTING PREPACKAGED SOFTWARE

For the immediate future the biggest advance in curriculum software will be adapting software packages designed for noneducational purposes, not by designing new programs.

Difficulties of Programming Special Educational Software

Starting from scratch to design and program your own educational software is an expensive and time-consuming effort. Theodore Ricks, director of electronic publishing at Harper and Row, says that about 300 hours of programming are needed to create one hour of computerized instruction. Developing a course on computers costs $50,000 to $100,000 and takes three to five years (Magarell, 1983e). Current prices for a copy of a computerized course are anywhere from $50 to $5,000, but in the next three years the increased volume of such material should bring the price down to $30 to $50 per course.

Frankly, most people do not have the skill for writing their own computerized courseware. Although faculty may be subject-matter experts, they are rarely experts in curriculum design and computer programming. Let's face it, most of us may be good in our subjects, but we are darn poor programmers and curriculum designers! And the existing "edu-

cational" software on the market generally shows this low level of expertise. Some professionally produced education packages exist, of course.
But most current educational software is mediocre in quality.

The "Adaptation" Strategy

So where *do* we get usable software? The biggest bang for the buck
will be prepackaged software originally designed for noneducational purposes. The strategy is simple: take word processing packages, business
accounting software, data base management systems, statistical packages,
financial spreadsheets, and other common noneducational software and
adapt it to the curriculum. For the near future *adaptation* will be the
highest payoff. Most of the so-called educational software is a sorry state
of affairs. But if you examine the noneducational packages with an eye to
curriculum adaptation the picture changes entirely. The programs are
widely available and have high quality.

Incidentally, effective use of prepackaged software is a clear example of what Charles Thomas, executive director of CAUSE, calls the
90/10 rule: 90 percent of the progress on any task is accomplished with 10
percent of the effort, but to move the last 10 percent to perfection requires
90 percent of the effort. *Adaptation* of noneducational software will obtain 90 percent of the effectiveness with only 10 percent of the effort compared to complete reprogramming. Undoubtedly we will eventually close
the gap with full scale computer-assisted instruction packages. In the
meantime we can have a tremendous impact, with small expenditures of
time and energy, by adapting noneducational software.

The Textbook/Lab Manual Approach

How will this adaptation occur? Probably with a "middle-man" lab
manual. For almost all courses there are standard *textbooks.* And for
many courses there are high-quality *noneducational software packages.*
A *lab manual* is needed to connect the two. This approach does not
require rewriting textbooks or the software. It simply requires a clever adaptation that links the software and the textbook. Of course, in the physical sciences the lab approach has been common for fifty years. Now is the
time to use the strategy creatively in the computer area.

Here is an example. Suppose you had a good sociology introductory
text and a good statistical package for a microcomputer. A good imagination could figure out how to design a lab manual that links the two. For example, suppose the lab manual's first exercise is for students to construct
a small questionnaire. After the questionnaire is constructed, critiqued
by the class, and carefully revised it could be administered to another
group of students. Incidentally, a word processing program will be invaluable in preparing that survey instrument. After the survey is
collected, the class could do many exercises using the statistical package
for analysis.

The beauty of this approach is that no adaptation of the textbook or the statistical package is necessary. This lab manual could be produced rather quickly. It does not need to be tied into one specific textbook or one specific statistical package. It could be keyed to many.

There are literally dozens of other opportunities for developing "middle-man" lab manuals:

1. Excellent existing accounting packages could be readily adapted to accounting textbooks.
2. Word processing programs could be widely used in English Composition and in any curriculum area that uses extensive writing.
3. Financial spreadsheets are ideal for management courses.
4. "Equation processors" (such as TK Solver) can be readily used in science and engineering courses.
5. Statistical packages could be used in many social science and natural science courses.
6. Data base management systems would be valuable in business and management courses.

Table 9-2 illustrates some software adaptation examples.

Advantages of the Software Adaptation Strategy

Compared to the software *production* strategy, the software *adaptation* approach has important advantages.

1. *Adaptation is much quicker than software production.* Starting from scratch with software is a slow, tedious, and expensive strategy. By contrast, adapting existing software can be extremely fast. The crying

---

TABLE 9-2. MICROCOMPUTER SOFTWARE FOR COLLEGE CURRICULA

Software for college curricula is rather scarce, but with a little imagination many commercial programs—not originally intended for education—can be adapted to educational purposes. The following are some examples:

Curriculum Area	Software Available
English Composition	Word processing
Social Sciences	Statistical packages
Physical Science	Many specially prepared packages
Business	Huge, sophisticated base of adaptable software
Remedial Education	Many specially prepared packages
Computer Science	Programming languages
Science and Engineering	"Equation processors"

need for more educational software can be partially met with this quick strategy, and students will not face the frustration of having machines but little software—a problem that has been dubbed "software burnout."

2. *Adaptation allows many textbooks to have a computer component.* When specially prepared software is designed for a single subject matter it is then limited to one textbook. Adaptation, however, allows a single piece of software and a manual to be keyed to many textbooks. This allows an "instant market" since users of the most popular textbooks would not have to abandon their favorites to use the computer lab manual. Thus, the decision to use the manual can be any easy "add-on" decision, not a more difficult "replacement" decision.

3. *Adaptation is very inexpensive compared to initial software production.* A publishing house can produce high-quality, useful adaptation manuals and books without the extremely high cost of software production.

4. *Widespread availability of adaptation books will in turn promote more use of microcomputers.* The chicken-and-the-egg cycle will be completed: the availability of computers has promoted software adaptation, and the availability of software adaptations will prompt wider use of the micros.

5. *Adaptation allows experts to capitalize on their specialties.* It is rare to find a person who can write software well, is a subject-matter expert, and knows enough about curriculum design to make the pieces fit. This is the unique combination needed to produce from-scratch software. By contrast, the *adaptation* strategy allows each player to capitalize on their strengths—the software expert simply writes good software, the textbook writer writes the textbook, and a third person applies curriculum design skills in producing the lab manual. In short, adaptation fosters an "experts-doing-their-best-thing" strategy.

The Entrepreneurial Connection: Can Adaptation Be Profitable?

We assume nobody is going to write or adapt software for education purposes if he or she cannot make money at it. No faculty member is going to take the time, no publishing house is going to stick its neck out, no software vendor is going to devote the resources unless they can translate those efforts into profits.

Persistent complaints have been aired in the popular software magazines and at educational conferences about the lack of profitability in educational software. The complaint is realistic—it is simply too easy to steal software, to copy disks, and to rob the maker of their rightful profits. At the recent conference of Computer Using Educators (CUE) in San Diego, for example, one major speaker made an impassioned plea for better self-discipline among educators. His point was simple: if educators keep stealing software, people will stop writing educational programs! We fully agree with his position.

However, the issue is conceived incorrectly from a business perspective. Right now most of the software is simply too expensive, thus tempting people to copy it. With the development of mass markets we expect software to come down radically in price, thus blunting the motive for copying it. But even more important, we think the business angle should simply be handled differently. The sale of textbooks is thoroughly entrenched in higher education, and few people bother to photocopy the textbook. They buy it. If the "lab manual" strategy were adopted the sale of the textbook could be the vehicle for recovering the software costs. The price of the disk would simply be incorporated into the lab manual or textbook. Given a mass market, and given the textbook as the pricing mechanism, we think that adaptation efforts can be commercially successful.

The commercial rule is simple: link the software to a textbook or lab manual. Then virtually give away the software, and make the profit on the book. This is a time-honored mechanism in higher education. It also has the important advantage of harnessing the creative efforts of the publishing industry. Publishers are important working partners in higher education and this partnership can be successfully applied to the computer revolution. In short, we think that publishers can and should make a profit; when they do they will plow development money back into the effort.

Incidentally, the same logic works for faculty members. Anyone who spends time and energy developing curricula should be rewarded, with royalties from the sales and with recognition and rewards from their home campus. Administrators who are serious about computer competency on their campuses will ensure that the leaders of the movement are well rewarded.

COMPUTER-ASSISTED INSTRUCTION

We have been emphasizing the adaptation of noneducational software. But what about the programs that are specifically designed as courseware, the computer-assisted instruction (CAI) packages? There have been, of course, many attempts to design a full curriculum, taught almost entirely by the computer. Unfortunately, CAI packages have tended to come in two stripes: questionable quality/low price, or excellent quality/outrageous price.

Qestionable Quality/Low Price

CAI packages do exist for micros, but generally they have been low-budget affairs programmed in somebody's family room on weekends —and the quality shows! Most of these packages were written for Apple

II's or Radio Shack equipment in the old eight-bit technology, using about 48K of memory. To put it another way, they were written in the lowest common denominator.

We are not trying to be cute. Obviously somebody put blood and sweat into some of these programs and did an admirable job considering budget and equipment limitations. And although these programs are usually poor, they were first tries and things should get better. The key problem was inadequate funding, a problem that should improve as the educational market enlarges. Anyone interested in a list of the better programs (among an admittedly weak field) should write for a catalog from CONDUIT, University of Iowa, P. O. Box 338, Iowa City, Iowa 52244.

PLATO: Excellent Quality/High Price

Control Data Corporation has spent twenty years of research and nearly a billion (that's right, BILLION) dollars to develop PLATO as one of the world's most comprehensive computer-based instructional programs. PLATO consists of over 8,000 hours of highly interactive, self-paced, one-to-one instruction. Over 1,200 lessons are offered by PLATO, ranging from personal development to nuclear physics. PLATO has been tested by more than 25,000 students in various settings and is now found in over 100 schools, colleges, and universities.

PLATO was originally developed in 1962 at the University of Illinois in cooperation with the National Science Foundation. PLATO courses initially were used to train Control Data personnel and were so successful that Control Data began to expand its courseware, leading to its present use in business, industry, government, and educational institutions throughout the world.

Two different versions of the PLATO system were originally available: the network-based system and a free-standing PLATO system. In the network-based system, several terminals are connected to a large central computer. These video-display terminals with typewriter keyboards present the lesson material on the screen in the form of text, drawings, and animated graphics. The student interacts with the computer by touching the screen at a specified place or by typing the appropriate response.

The free-standing PLATO system allows PLATO lessons to be delivered independent of a central computer. This is achieved through the Control Data 110 microcomputer that uses a microprocessor in the terminal and an off-line flexible disk drive. This microcomputer, then, uses courseware contained on the disks and can be hooked up with a modem to the central system if more lessons, testing, or record keeping is required.

Recently, Control Data has begun to offer some of its courseware for other microcomputers. The Apple II Plus, Atari 800, and Texas Instruments 99/4A microcomputers were selected. The IBM PC has also been discussed as a target machine. The first nine lessons presented are: Basic Number Facts, Whole Numbers, Decimals, Fractions, Physical Engineering: Elementary Mechanics, French Vocabulary Builder, German Vocabulary Builder, Spanish Vocabulary Builder, and Computer Literacy: Introduction. In the near future, the following courseware will also be available for microcomputers: Life Coping Skills Series, Computer Literacy Curriculum, and Computer Concepts. The Digital Equipment Company has recently purchased a substantial block of PLATO courses for reconfiguration on its Rainbow and Professional 300 microcomputer series. For further information on microcomputer courseware contact: Control Data Publishing Co., P. O. Box 261127, San Diego, California 92126.

PLATO's problem has been a breath-taking price tag. Control Data dropped nearly a billion dollars into PLATO—and sometimes it seems they want to get it all back from *your* lease! Until recently PLATO was available only on mainframes and the charge was stiff. And campuses rarely *replaced* personnel costs; instead the cost of PLATO was on *top* of personnel. Thus PLATO was widely judged "too expensive." Well, that depends. If PLATO is an add-on cost, with no personnel efficiencies, it is expensive. On the other hand, if more students can be taught for the same personnel costs it would not seem so costly. If you can introduce personnel savings in growing areas (so staff will not have to be *replaced*) the political acceptability will be higher.

In addition, the microcomputer versions of PLATO may provide a real price breakthrough. At this point not enough microcomputer PLATO is available to judge. Anyone interested in CAI should keep their eyes peeled for developments on the PLATO horizon.

Authoring Languages

Integrating CAI into the classroom is sometimes difficult because the courseware does not parallel the topics that the instructor feels are relevant. Handouts, dittos, and lab exercises that are supplementary to the standard textbook have long been a standard in most classrooms. Understandably, instructors are eager to draw upon their own knowledge and experience in creating instructional tools. Many instructors will be reluctant to use the computer as an instructional tool unless they can tailor-make computer programs to fulfill their specific needs.

Until recently, designing computer courseware required the expertise of a programmer and many long hours in the tedious task of writing code. Most teachers do not have time to become programming experts and certainly cannot afford to hire a programmer to write software. *Authoring languages,* however, are designed to short-circuit this problem by providing teachers with an easy way to write their own instructional programs.

Authoring programs such as PILOT, PASS, Scholar/Teach3 and

PLANIT are user-friendly programs with a predetermined instructional methodology built into them. Many authoring languages include instructional features such as graphic capabilities, answer analysis, branching, review options, author comments, hinting, scoring, and "help" functions.

Some authoring systems, e.g. PASS, make it easy for instructors to design their own courseware by making the program self-prompting, menu-driven, and English based. Thus, the lesson designer can concentrate on lesson development rather than computer programming. Many authoring systems will also interface with peripherals such as slide projectors or video tapes that can greatly enrich the instructional program. For specific information on these authoring systems, contact the following companies:

PASS: Photo and Sound Co., 1425 Koll Circle, #110, San Jose, CA 95112, (408) 293-9610.

Scholor/Teach3: Boeing Computer Services Co., Education and Training Dividsion, 5757 W. Century Blvd, Suite 401 W. Los Angeles, CA 90045, (213) 417-5010.

PLANIT: System Development Corporation, Human Systems Division, Santa Monica, CA 90406, (213) 820-4111.

PILOT, SUPERPILOT: Contact your local Apple Dealer.

RESEARCH ON THE EFFECTIVENESS OF COMPUTERS IN THE CURRICULUM

Educators have recently been asked to justify the vast expenditure for this new computer technology. Educational software and hardware are the fastest growing segments of the personal-computer market. According to figures from Market Data Retrieval, the number of classroom computers in U. S. public schools tripled from 1981 to 1983. In addition, a study by the Eastern Management Group predicts that the 250,000 systems that now exist in U. S. schools will increase tenfold by 1990! Educational software sales are also expected to jump from their present $60 million per year to $900 million annually within the next five years. Given this growing interest in educational computers, what is known about their *effectiveness*? Is there any evidence to show that computers increase *student learning*?

Research on CAI

Recent research attempting to answer these questions is encouraging, although incomplete. Current studies have still not identified the critical elements that lead to a successful computer-assisted instruction program. Two major studies have reviewed the literature in CAI and concluded that (1) CAI does increase student achievement; (2) CAI significantly decreased the time needed for mastery; and (3) CAI increases positive attitudes toward both the computer and the subject matter. The first study was conducted by the Office of Technology Assessment (1982) and the other by Kulik, Bangert, and Williams (1983).

Four reasons are suggested for the increased interest in computers in education. A recent report by the Office of Technology Assessment mentions:

1. Computer hardware has rapidly decreased in price, making it *affordable* to schools and parents.
2. The *rising cost of labor* makes computers an attractive alternative to the traditional labor intensive classroom.
3. Developments in instructional design encourage exploration of this growing technology.
4. The ability to link the computer to *other technologies* such as videodisk and cable television offer even greater possibilities for instruction.

The Office of Technology Assessment report reviews several CAI studies and concludes that "there is a substantial amount of agreement that, for many educational applications, information technology can be an effective and economic tool for instruction."

Research shows the positive effects of CAI. Kulik and his associates (1983) reviewed 301 studies analyzing CAI effectiveness in grades 6 through 12. They were forced to reject some 250 studies due to serious methodological flaws. The remaining 51 evaluations, however, shared many conclusions. Results indicated that CAI *raised student scores* on final examinations from the 50th to the 63rd percentile. There were also positive effects on scores in a follow-up examination given to students several months later, although the increases were not as dramatic as the immediate effects of CAI. In addition, students using CAI *developed positive attitudes* toward the computer as well as the course content. Last, CAI significantly *reduced the learning time* students needed.

Kulik, Kulik, and Cohen (1980) analyzed the results of many studies on computer-based college teaching. The results were consistent with the above findings, although the effects were not as dramatic.

Other studies confirm the findings. Chambers and Sprecher's 1980 review of the literature came to the following conclusions on the effectiveness of CAI:

1. CAI either improved learning or showed no difference when compared to the traditional classroom approach.
2. CAI improved student attitudes toward computers in learning.
3. Faculty are more likely to accept and use CAI materials if the materials are developed according to specific guidelines.

More research is needed to settle the question. An implicit assumption in many CAI studies is that a homogeneous effect comes from com-

---

ADVANTAGES OF CAI

1. CAI provides individualized instruction through custom self-tailored learning paths.
2. CAI is self-paced and available 24 hours a day, 7 days a week (computers don't take vacations).
3. Immediate feedback is given to the learner.
4. Mistakes become a learning rather than a punishing experience.
5. A nonthreatening environment is created wherein the student can feel free to access exactly what is needed. It is less intimidating to ask a computer time-consuming details than to ask the teacher. With CAI the students can take *thier* time rather than the time of others.
6. Simulation is possible. Experimenting with alternatives aids total comprehension.
7. Audio interaction is possible with speech synthesis.
8. Hours of grading and scoring can be eliminated.
9. Courseware can build in a test validity study for use in course improvement.

---

puters as instructional tools. In fact, the effect of computers in education is diverse, just as the effect of textbooks or slide presentations is diverse. Students do not learn from the computer itself any more than they learn from a slide projector. The instructional design and content of the slides facilitate learning. Similarly, it is the instructional content and design of the computer software that promotes learning rather than the actual computer. Unfortunately, most studies have isolated only the computer as the critical variable rather than *how the computer is being used.*

Criteria for Judging CAI

The market for educational software is rapidly expanding, thus arousing the interest of major companies in the software, publishing, and entertainment business. Educators must become critical and discriminating in their software purchases to ensure quality educational programs.

Recent research in learning psychology has provided some useful criteria to be considered when purchasing educational software. Some elements to consider in top-quality educational programs are:

1. Does the program allow the student to be an *active* participant in learning rather than a passive observer? Does it encourage students to use their prior knowledge and experiences to construct meaning and thus understanding from the material?
2. Is the *control* with the student rather than with the computer?
3. Is the *feedback* in the form of information rather than of evaluation?

4. Does the program help develop *critical thinking* instead of rote learning?
5. Does the program guide the student toward eventual *success* and *mastery* over the material?
6. Does the program diagnose students and provide them with material based on their particular *needs*?

CAREER GUIDANCE AND MICROCOMPUTERS

With the advent of microcomputers, several educational testing agencies created computerized interactive career guidance programs. DISCOVER, by the American College Testing Service, is one example. Another popular guidance program is SIGI which is described below as excerpted from a bulletin by the Educational Testing Service (Katz, 1981).

What is Sigi?*

SIGI (pronounced Siggy) is a computer-based System of Interactive Guidance and Information designed to help students in two-year and four-year colleges make career decisions. It has been developed at ETS with the help of grants from the Carnegie Corporation, the National Science Foundation, and the Kellogg Foundation.

SIGI is based on a humanistic philosophy, a theory of guidance that emphasizes individual values, a vast store of occupational data, and a strategy for processing information—all blended into a unified system.

Students who are at different stages in career decision making may use SIGI in distinctive ways. Each student presents a unique combination of values, interests, abilities, preceptions, preferences, and plans. Each student, therefore, requires unique treatment. Yet there are common elements in the process of making career decisions. SIGI provides a clearly defined structure of decision making for all students, but responds flexibly to individual needs and circumstances.

What Does Sigi Try to Accomplish?

The main purposes of SIGI are to increase students' freedom of choice, and to improve their competence in the process of making informed and rational career decisions. In this process, they examine their own values searchingly, explore options systematically, interpret relevant data accurately, and formulate tentative plans as hypotheses that can be tested realistically. They also learn to modify their plans as they gain new insights, experience, and information.

The choices directly considered include educational and occupational options. SIGI does not, however, pretend to ensure the "right" choice for every student—except insofar as the right choice is defined as an informed and rational choice. In short, SIGI aims to help students master strategies

*From the SIGI Information Bulletin. Educational Testing Service, Princeton, New Jersey. Reprinted by permission.

for rational behavior in the face of uncertainty. It helps them to learn what information they need, to get what information they want, and to use what information they have.

How Does Sigi Work?

Each student interacts with the system via a cathode-ray tube (CRT) terminal. The terminal consists of a screen and an array of response keys. Messages, called frames, are presented (or constructed) on the screen, and the student responds to a question, asks a question, or gives directions to the computer by pressing designated keys. Sometimes the screen gives information to the student. Sometimes it gives the student choices of what to do next. Sometimes it serves as a spokesman for the student, who may try out and modify various expressions of his or her own values, specifications of minimum requirements, and occupational goals and plans.

The student's dialogue with the system about career decisions takes place in a multiple-choice format. This format candidly and explicitly specifies the structure of the system to students, yet permits them to branch through a multiplicity of pathways within that structure. It instructs them in the rules and possibilities of the decision-making process, but allows them to make the decisions for themselves.

Each student proceeds at his or her own pace. Scripts are written for the eighth-grade level of reading, but slow readers have been able to use SIGI—it simply takes them longer. Most students spend three to four hours at the terminal (usually spread over two or three sessions), although some will use considerably more.

SIGI® AT A GLANCE

- ☐ is an interactive computer-based aid to career decision making . . .
- ☐ serves primarily students in, or about to enter, two-year and four-year colleges . . .
- ☐ complements the work of guidance counselors . . .
- ☐ was developed on the PDP-11 computer . . .
- ☐ has been converted for other minicomputers, some mainframes, and certain microcomputers . . .
- ☐ includes six interrelated subsystems listed below. (Each subsystem raises a major question and helps the student answer it. These questions and answers form distinctive steps in decision making.)

Subsystem	What the Student Does	Questions Answered
Introduction	Learns concepts and uses of major sections listed below.	Where do you stand now in your career decision making? What help do you need?
I. VALUES	Examines 10 occupational values and weights importance of each one.	What satisfactions do you want in an occupation? What are you willing to give up?

II. LOCATE	Puts in specifications on 5 values at a time and gets lists of occupations that meet specifications.	Where can you find what you want? What occupations should you look into?
III. COMPARE	Asks pointed questions and gets specific information about occupations of interest.	What would you like to know about occupations that you are considering? Should you reduce your list?
IV. PREDICTION	Finds out probabilities of getting various marks in key courses of preparatory programs for occupations.	Can you make the grade? What are your chances of success in preparing for each occupation you are considering?
V. PLANNING	Gets displays of program for entering each occupation, licensing or certification requirements, and sources of financial aid.	How do you get from here to there? What steps do you take to enter an occupation you are considering?
VI. STRATEGY	Evaluates occupations in terms of the rewards they offer and the risks of trying to enter them.	Which occupations fit your values best? How do you decide between an occupation that is highly desirable but risky and one that is less desirable but easier to prepare for?

The computer records everything that each student tells it and keeps track of every branch that each student follows. As students progress, they learn to move freely within the structure of SIGI and eventually gain control of the system to use as they see fit. . . .

Why Was Sigi Designed Primarily for Colleges?

Although SIGI is adaptable to other settings and populations, two-year and four-year colleges appear to combine great need and readiness for it.

Colleges have generally expressed a strong commitment to providing career guidance for all students, and the students themselves have indicated their urgent need for intensive help in career decision making. Yet career guidance services have been found to lag behind the need. Even in the most favored institutions, there are usually at least 300 students to a counselor. The counselors have many duties besides career guidance. At the same time, colleges have tended to be open to new ideas and have especially welcomed innovative uses of technology.

Many colleges have made SIGI terminals available to high school students and to the community at large. These outreach programs have provided substantial benefits to the colleges as well as to those clienteles. . . .

Will Sigi Replace Counselors?

SIGI is planned to fit into the regular career guidance programs at the colleges. It will not supplant counselors. Rather, it will complement the work of the guidance staff.

SIGI does superbly some things that human counselors cannot do efficiently, or at all. It stores, retrieves instantly, and manipulates vast amounts of information, putting great resources at the fingertips of each student, tailored to his or her individual needs. It brings together many sets of variables—personal, occupational, and institutional. By combining these sets of variables in distinctive ways for each student, it constructs new and unique information—as illustrated in the description of "Locate," "Prediction," and "Strategy."

On the other hand, SIGI does not attempt to do what many counselors do superbly. It does not provide a warm human relationship; it does not try to solve personal, social, or academic problems; it does not attempt to cope with emotional upsets.

There are, however, ways in which the counselor's work may articulate quite closely with SIGI. The "Counselor's Handbook for SIGI" suggests how the counselor can capitalize on students' experience with SIGI. SIGI may stir up concerns which the student will want to discuss with the counselor. Furthermore, while SIGI deals with occupational decisions, it does not include placement into specific local jobs within an occupation. A counselor or placement officer may apply many of the SIGI paradigms in assisting students to choose and seek jobs within each locality. Thus, working together, the counselor and SIGI can help students much more than either could manage independently. In short, SIGI has been found to increase the productivity of counselors.

WHERE TO FIND EDUCATIONAL SOFTWARE

Many educators face a serious stumbling block: where to find good educational software? Many administrators often complain that after obtaining hardware, setting up the lab, and encouraging faculty to implement computers in the curriculum, they are embarrassed by the scarcity of educational software in various subject areas. If faculty members use computers in their courses they need to know about software and how it can be utilized.

Many efforts to develop educational software have been launched across the nation, from software vendors to publishing companies to creative instructional designers. Unfortunately, there is no coordinated national effort to evaluate and disseminate information on educational software from these various sources.

Electronic Data Base Searches

Recent developments in large data bases offer hope to this pervasive problem. A moderate membership fee, a computer, and a modem enable educators to conduct a software search. Two companies, *Datapro* and *Softsearch*, provide this new service. Although neither data base has a comprehensive list of educational programs, they are a useful starting point and will probably become a standard method for finding software. (Datapro's address is Datapro, 1805 Underwood Blvd., Delram, New Jersey 08075.) Let's look more closely at one of these, Softsearch.

Softsearch maintains one of the largest commercial software data bases in the world. Over 30,000 programs are on file for micro, mini, and mainframe computers. This particular data base does not require the user to have a computer and modem to conduct a search. Instead, the user calls Softsearch with the specific criteria they need. This locator service will then find the software products that match the user's specifications. Softsearch runs the request against their computer data base and a custom report is sent to the user within forty-eight hours.

Users can obtain a single search or may subscribe to Softsearch and receive five reports. The reports also include a manual, user's guide, and evaluation checklist. Each report is a one-page information sheet that includes (1) the product name; (2) a description; (3) the vendor's name; address, sales contact, and telephone number; (4) institutions served; (5) operating system requirements; (6) source languages; (7) number of current users; and (8) pricing information. Currently 1,000 computer-based instructional programs are on line with Softsearch and nearly 3,000 educational institutions and libraries use the service. For information, call toll free 1-800-334-2122 or write to Softsearch International, Inc., P. O. Box 5276, San Antonio, Texas 78201.

Software Guides

A source for information on educational software for the Apple computer is *Swift's Educational Software Directory*. Swift's lists the educational software offered by publishers, software houses, and noncommercial software sources. The directory describes each program, its price, its publishers, its grade level, its memory requirements, and its language requirements. The directory also cites reviews, where available, to help educators decide if the program will meet their requirements. For information write to Sterling Swift Publishing Company, 1600 Fortview Road, Austin, Texas 78704.

A manual published by Apple called "The Book" provides a broader guide to software. The Book is a listing of programs broke down by areas such as business, entertainment, education, graphics, accounting, and so forth. This guide gives the price, publisher, memory requirements, description, and a short evaluation. Where more than one program is available in an area (such as data base management or word processing), a comparative evaluation is conducted across all programs to help clarify the available features.

Another guide that provides an extremely good source list and evaluation of education software is the 1983 Educational Software Preview Guide. This guide was developed by the Educational Software Evaluation Consortium, representing seventeen educational organizations throughout North America. The selection of programs in this guide is based on critical evaluation conducted by the participating organizations, the California Software Evaluation Forum, and some reviews published in professional journals. The guide contains over 200 programs indexed by curriculum area, topic, cost, and computer brand. For information write: California TEC Center, Software Library and Clearinghouse, SMERC Library, San Mateo County Office of Education, 333 Main Street, Redwood City, California 94063.

Nonprofit Organizations

A number of nonprofit organizations provide software information for education. Here are three.

Conduit is a nonprofit organization supported by the National Science Foundation and the Fund for the Improvement of Postsecondary Education. It promotes instructional computing in colleges and universities by disseminating instructional materials and information. Conduit not only develops its own educational programs but will also disseminate software programs written by individuals, if the programs meet their evaluation criteria. All programs are reviewed and field-tested by educators experienced in the particular content area. Once the program has passed the review process, the Conduit staff then configures the program for use on a variety of computers. For more information on the available educational programs write Conduit, University of Iowa, P. O. Box 338, Iowa City, Iowa 52244.

The Minnesota Educational Computing Consortium (MECC) was established in 1973 to assist Minnesota schools and colleges in implementing educational computing. MECC offers many services including the development and distribution of microcomputer courseware. Major emphasis has been placed on curricular materials for the Apple II and Atari 400 microcomputers. MECC has approximately 200 educational programs available which have been distributed to hundreds of educational institutions throughout the nation. They also have curriculum guides to help implement computer use in the classroom. Nonprofit educational institutions outside Minnesota may obtain annual service agreements with MECC that grant MECC courseware at reduced prices.

For more information write or call MECC, Institutional Memberships, 2520 Broadway Drive, St. Paul, Minnesota 55113, (612) 638-0611.

Computer Using Educators (CUE) is another nonprofit corporation. CUE is affiliated with the International Council for Computer Education which was developed to promote and improve computer usage in educational institutions. CUE presently has over 5,000 members from across the nation. One of CUE's many services is an educational software library and exchange called SOFTSWAP. SOFTSWAP takes contributed programs from educators and organizes them onto disks that are sold for $10 each, with permission to copy freely. A catalog listing hundreds of programs available for Apple, Atari, Compucolor, PET, and TRS-80 may be obtained by contacting Ann Lathrop, SMERC Library, San Mateo County Office of Education, 333 Main Street, Redwood City, California 94063.

Other information on resources is included in the accompanying box.

BUILDING A CURRICULUM FOCAL POINT

Who will spearhead the campus-wide computer efforts? Obviously your computer specialists will play a major role in the effort. That is why computer center directors, computer staffs, and computer science departments exist. But simply reinforcing the priesthood and true believers is not enough. The general curriculum needs help and that requires enlisting the help of people other than the computer specialists.

The Need for a Spearhead Department

Our experience suggests that many scholarly departments will move rapidly into using microcomputers. But to penetrate the curriculum, to move into the general education program, usually requires one or two "focal" departments. An ideal focal department will have three characteristics:

1. faculty and students in that department will not have much experience with computers, thus breaking the traditional mode about who controls computing ("By golly, if the English Department can do it so can I!");
2. the department should have a major role in the general education program; and
3. the faculty should be eager to participate (there is no sense dragging unwilling faculty into the activity).

The focal department's identity, then, will depend upon unique circumstances in each college or university. We have seen many different

EDUCATIONAL COMPUTING: MAGAZINES AND NEWSLETTERS FOR UP-TO-DATE INFORMATION

The magazines and newsletters listed below contain current useful information for educators in the computing world. Although the list is not comprehensive, it definitely provides some excellent sources.

ACM Sigcue Bulletin
Association for Computing Machinery
P.O. Box 12015
Church Street Station
New York, New York 10249

Apple Education News
Apple Computer, Inc.
Mail Stop 18-C
20525 Mariani Avenue
Cupertino, CA 95014
(Subscriptions free.)

Classroom Computer News
341 Mt. Auburn Street
Watertown, MA 02172

Collegiate Microcomputer
Rose-Hulman Institute of Technology
Terre Haute, IN 47803

Communication Outlook
Artificial Language Laboratory
Computer Science Department
Michigan State University
East Lansing, MI 48824

Computers & Education: An International Journal
Pergamon Press, Inc.
Maxwell House, Fairview Park
Elmsford, NY 10523

The Computing Teacher
Department of Computer and Information Science
University of Oregon
Eugene, OR 97403

Creative Computing
P.O. Box 789-M
Morristown, NJ 07950

C.U.E. Newsletter
Computer Using Educators
P.O. Box 18547
San Jose, CA 95158

Educational Computer
P.O. Box 535
Cupertino, CA 95015

Educational Technology
140 Sylvan Avenue
Englewood Cliffs, NJ 07632

Electronic Education
Suite 220
1311 Executive Center Drive
Tallahassee, FL 32301

Electronic Learning
902 Sylvan Avenue
Englewood Cliffs, NJ 07632

Instructional Innovator
Association for Educational Communications and Technology
1126 Sixteenth Street, NW
Washington, D.C. 20036

The Journal of Courseware Review
The Foundation for the Advancement of Computer-Aided Education
Available at Apple Dealerships and some bookstores.

Microcomputers in Education
5 Chapel Hill Drive
Fairfield, CT 06432

T.H.E. Journal
P.O. Box 992
Acton, MA 01720

Users
MECC
2520 Broadway Drive
St. Paul, MN 55113

Window
469 Pleasant Street
Watertown, MA 02172
(Disk-based magazine)

selections. At Chapman College, the English department was selected as the focal group, and they penetrated the general education program with word processing. At the College of Notre Dame, the Business Administration department developed microcomputer courses for the general education curriculum. At Lambuth College, the sociology department developed an introduction to sociology and simultaneously to statistics, using a microcomputer statistics package. Successful colleges were able to enlist one or two departments outside the computer specialists to spearhead the effort.

More Than One Spearhead Department?

It is wise to pick at least two focal departments. There is no guarantee that any given department will muster the enthusiasm and effort to translate their initial eagerness into long-term course development. It probably makes sense to hedge your bet by having at least two departments working on computer spearhead efforts. For example, try a combination of an English program using word processing and a Social Science department using statistics.

A General Education Course

What will the focal departments do? First, they should develop a general education, mass appeal course that uses microcomputers extensively. (Of course, a microcomputer lab that provides full access to machines is mandatory.) Probably this introductory course should be team-taught. The work load is too much for a single person to adapt the course as a vehicle for computer literacy as well as teach it for its traditional purposes. The purpose is to kill two birds with one stone, both to teach the traditional subject matter in some important course and to integrate computer literacy.

Remember, avoid setting up "special" computer literacy classes and instead spread the computer literacy activities throughout the curriculum mainstream. Thus, the course will not be entitled "Computer Literacy Basics 101." It will be called English Composition 101" as it always has been. But here is the new twist: the *English professors* will be teaching basic computer literacy integrated into that course. We are looking for integration, not specialization; for use by noncomputer specialists, not only by the Priesthood; for burying computer literacy in the heart of the curriculum, not singling it out for special courses.

What should this focal course include? Certainly it should cover the standard subjects of that course—English Composition, Sociology, or whatever. And it should at least cover the same five softwares we specified for staff training—utilities, word processing, data base management, graphics, and budget spreadsheets. Of course, integrating this much microcomputer activity into a basic course will require more time for the course, expanded quarters or semesters, or expanded credit units.

Other Steps: Training and Expansion

As the basic course is developed the faculty in the focal department should have more elaborate training. The focal department will certainly need more intensive training than the general campus-wide program.

The initial course and the faculty training are the first steps. A spearhead department will then try to incorporate microcomputers throughout its curriculum. Earlier we mentioned both the computer-assisted instruction approach and the "textbook/lab manual" approach. The spearhead department should examine both strategies and develop courses that implement them. At this stage departments will have to develop many of their own materials, but in a few years such adapted curriculum courseware will be readily available.

EXPANDING TO OTHER CURRICULUM AREAS

Once the computer literacy program is firmly established in some large general education courses, an effort should be made to expand into other areas. What are some likely candidates? Recently, TALMIS, a consulting service in Illinois, conducted a survey of 607 colleges and university faculty members who use microcomputers (Magarrell, 1983d). The survey found a wide range of usage among the various academic disciplines. For instance, education departments used microcomputers most in teaching courses of computer literacy. The liberal arts departments are using the microcomputers for drill and practice and word processing. Even library course instructors are finding uses for the microcomputer in searching computerized collections of information. And of course, teaching programming classes is one of the highest uses of the microcomputer by faculty members.

The following chart illustrates how the faculty members surveyed used microcomputers:

A *Teaching*		B *Personal Use*	
Mathematical		Word processing	53%
computation	60%	Computation	45%
Simulation	46%	Record keeping	34%
Presenting instruction	42%	Recreation	33%
Teaching computer		Creating teaching	
literacy	42%	programs	32%
Teaching programming	41%	Graphics	27%
Drill and practice	33%	Accounting	12%
Word processing	30%		
Graphics	25%		
Searches of data bases	21%		
Testing	19%		
Educational games	12%		
Research and other	5%		

Computers and the Liberal Arts

Everyone knows, of course, that computers are essential in the science, math, and engineering curricula. But what about computers in the liberal arts? On June 30, 1983, the *Wall Street Journal* ran an article on Carnegie-Mellon University, an institution with strong reputation in the "hard" sciences. At Carnegie-Mellon, however, a strong effort is being directed at computers in the liberal arts. Despite some reservations, the liberal arts faculty are gradually being won over. Listen to some of the comments in the *Journal* article (Carey, 1983):

> The faculty should "forget all this philosophical talk about what is liberal arts," says Preston Covey, director of the philosophy program. "Whether we like it or not, computers have entered the fray. As humanists, we need to understand this phenomenon. It's a tool that will have impact."
>
> A few Carnegie-Mellon professors who already use computers to teach arts and humanities contend that the machines reduce the need for boring classroom drills, reinforce skills such as writing and analysis, and better prepare students for jobs.
>
> "To me, it's a kind of golden age," says Katherine Lynch, an assistant professor of history. "Students can take tests on the computer to master the factual materials so we can go on to the interesting stuff—interpretation, discussion on issues, paper writing—in class."
>
> In the music department, students already do some of their drill work with computers. For ear training, they can practice in the solfege lab, where a computer plays a series of notes and the student types in the pitches.
>
> "The students love it," says Marilyn Thomas, an assistant professor. "It's another computer toy. And it gives them extra work in problem areas without tutors.". . .
>
> In the art and design departments, computer use has grown dramatically in the past two years. "There were writers before Gutenberg and painters after photography was introduced," says Warren Wake, an assistant professor of design. "Computers don't change the need for creativity."
>
> With programs that produce paint shades, type faces and other graphic parts, students can make new creations while learning how to use the technology, he says. Enrollment in the elective course, "Introduction to Computer Graphics," has grown fourfold since it began, Mr. Wake says, because students from such fields as engineering, statistics and communications are signing up.
>
> Lynda Ferris, a 22-year-old art major who will graduate next spring with a degree in drawing, is glad she took two computer art courses. Thanks to them, she has a job this summer teaching the creative staff of a New Jersey advertising promotions company how to use computer-graphics programs.
>
> Students in the drama department are learning stage lighting on a computer system and are writing plays on terminals. "They used to use Scotch tape and throw paper on the floor," says Mr. Midani, the fine-arts dean. "But the act of constructing a dramatic text is beautifully suited to a computer's word-processing ability."
>
> Two freshman-level history courses already use computers. In one,

"Origins of the Modern World," students studying the factors that led to the French Revolution use the computer to look at grievances submitted to Louis XVI by French citizens. "The skills and learning aren't new," says Miss Lynch, "but the computer helps make quantitative data meaningful."

Freeing Class Time

Mr. Covey has developed computer exercises that philosophy students can do on their own to learn formal logic notations. That frees class time, he says, for discussing public policy and social issues.

The English department has applied for a foundation grant to start a writing-skills center that would use computer drills. David Kaufer, an assistant professor who wrote the grant proposal, says drills are a much more efficient way than classroom work to teach and reinforce basic writing skills.

SUMMARY

We assume that in a few years almost every department in a college or university will have some courses that depend heavily on computers. Table 9-1 identified six major ways in which computers are used in the curriculum.

A campus that plans to spend its computer efforts campus-wide will put several components into place. First, it will ensure widespread *access* to computers through computer laboratories, faculty and staff purchase plans, and student purchases. Second, a substantial effort in *faculty and staff training* is an essential ingredient in a successful program. Third, careful attention to *networking needs* between microcomputers and larger computers is important. Fourth, an effective program will find a *curriculum focal point* in the general education program. Fifth, the campus will build on the *traditional strengths* of the computer science areas and the traditional users such as math and science. Finally, computer usage will gradually *spread across the curriculum*. Nothing will occur suddenly or without pain. But with energy and resources a campus can move rapidly into the computer era and better prepare its students for a future that is at our doorstep.

One of the future developments is *interactive video,* a combination of computer and video disk technology. This promising development is discussed in Appendix B.

CHAPTER 10

NETWORKING

As we held workshops and mini conferences around the country, we noticed an interesting shift in the discussions. Before 1983 most of the debate centered on *whether* to use microcomputers on the campus; from 1983 on the debate was *how* best to incorporate microcomputers. One of the key "how" questions revolves around networking.

THE TREND TOWARD NETWORKING

The basic concept of networking is deceptively simple: several machines are wired together. They share central files and equipment such as printers, tape drives, and hard disks. Unfortunately, in addition to that basic simple concept, there are some rather complex ideas.

Why Networks?

Several reasons govern the trend toward networking. Here is a quotation from Harry Saal, of Westar Systems, a company specializing in networking. Saal explains some of the motivation for networks.

> The ideal state of computing—in which any computer or office device can communicate with any other device—is still on the horizon. By sharing information between physically separated personal computers, corporate computers, expensive printers, and disk drives, networking is becoming more feasible and desirable every working day.
>
> Often the information that managers would like to analyze with their electronic spreadsheet programs is ready and waiting on databases on the company mainframe computer, waiting for an easy communications link to the workspace in the managers' desk-top computers. Electronic mail will help usher in a new era of office productivity, improving inter-company communications and ending vicious circles of returning calls to people who've returned your calls, etc.

138

Systems of computers and peripherals linked together in adjacent offices and buildings, or local area networks (LAN's), will bring about complete office automation and standardize computer inter-connections. But we're not quite there, yet. . . .

Although often separated by distance, allied users must work together cooperatively. On different floors, in different buildings, or in different states and countries, fellow workers must exchange information. For them, communications are no longer a luxury; they are essential and growing daily in importance.

Two recent developments, local area networking and personal computing, provide a way to address the needs of this new class of computer users. Community microcomputing is the merger of these two technologies.

Community microcomputing enables a community of users to share information that resides on common peripherals. Users share common programs and data as well as expensive, high-quality equipment such as printers and disks. Individuals connected to a community microcomputing system have their own dedicated personal computers as well as support environments for communications and for sharing of peripherals and information. Familiar personal computers, serving as desk-top workstations, provide a non threatening setting that enhances the effectiveness of professional and clerical workers. These personal workstations are open-ended, multifunction tools that make possible work processing, data manipulation, graphics, and sending electronic messages [Saal 1983, pp. 60–61].

Much Talk, Less Action

Although the concept is relatively simple, networking microcomputers has not yet become a common practice. The procedure is fairly expensive, usually costing between $500 and $1,000 per machine, sometimes much more. Moreover, the whole thrust of microcomputers has been away from centralized computing toward individual users who can function alone. In some sense networking goes against the grain of the philosophy behind microcomputing. Most important, networking has not spread widely because many people have found that they simply do not need it. For many functions, microcomputers work well independently. When you consider the full cost of networking and then contrast that with the convenience of stand-alone microcomputing, the decision is often to buy more printers and peripheral equipment rather than to share them through networking.

Nevertheless, in spite of their relatively infrequent use up to the present, most observers expect networks to be more common in the future. The prices will undoubtedly come down, electronic mail will become more common, and the shared facilities of the network will look more attractive.

Networking roughly breaks into three functional types: (1) local area networks; (2) host/micro networks; and (3) micro to information base. From a technical point of view, two and three are the same, but they look quite different to the user. Let us examine the three types.

LOCAL AREA NETWORKS

When a cluster of microcomputers are wired up among themselves to share central files and equipment the result is a local area network (LAN). A typical configuration might include six microcomputers, one of which is the "server" that controls traffic on the network. The server also manages the peripheral equipment, which consists of a letter quality printer, a hard disk, and a graphics plotter. The hard disk holds mass storage for the network, especially data that all the different users must access.

This arrangement would be satisfactory for a small office situation, such as the registrar of a small college. The hard disk, if big enough, could hold the records that everyone needed for access and updating. In addition, the independent microcomputers could provide stand-alone capacity for word processing, budget spreadsheets, graphics, and other operations. Finally, the peripherals could be shared among the users on the network.

Promises and Problems with a Local Area Network

Why would anyone want this network? Many good reasons exist, but unfortunately difficulties must also be carefully considered.

1. *Local area networks allow some advantages of sharing, but they maintain the important stand-alone features of microcomputing.* Contrast this LAN setup with the traditional "big computer with terminals" approach. The key advantage is that each user has a real computer, can do important work in a decentralized fashion, can control the process, and can use the machine when he or she wishes. In other words, the LAN allows the important advantages of microcomputing, contrasting sharply with the terminal that is dependent on a host computer.

2. *The LAN allows several microcomputers to share the same data base.* Often many people need the same data, and it may be updated frequently. Of course, data could be shared by passing around floppy disks, but this procedure has two important flaws. First, the floppies do not hold much information. Second, the floppies are likely to be out of date or inconsistent because multiple copies are floating around. By contrast to the floppies, a network with a hard disk for storage of shared files is a real advantage.

However, the problem with file sharing is the lack of security. Everyone on the network can share the hard disk, and many LANs have very weak security. If you maintain very sensitive files an LAN may be more vulnerable than you can tolerate, especially the less expensive systems.

3. *The LAN may allow users to share expensive programs.* Some programs can be placed on the hard disk and shared by all the users on the network. This could save money.

However, be alert, Many popular programs will *not* run on a hard disk. Moreover, if they run, the manufacturer will probably charge more for a multi-user version of the program, thus cutting into your potential savings. Demand to see the software *working* on your system!

4. *The LAN allows users to share expensive peripherals.* Examples of equipment that would justify networking are letter quality printers, hard disk drives, and plotters.

Networks are probably not justified for inexpensive equipment such as floppy disk drives and dot matrix printers. In small offices it is sometimes more cost effective to buy additional peripherals instead of buying networking capabilities.

5. *The LAN allows for electronic communication among users.* There is much discussion about the new era of "electronic mail," and for some situations it can be very helpful. With electronic networking important information can be instantaneously available for everyone on the network.

However, we worry a little about the problems of electronic junk mail that can be produced with easy facility on the computer. Moreover, there is a simple practical question. Do you really need electronic mail among the few users that an LAN is supposed to serve? By definition, an LAN serves a small geographic area; could that area be served easily with older techniques?

6. *An LAN might be useful in a teaching laboratory.* Sharing files, programs, and storage might be valuable in the classroom situation. Classwork problems could be mounted in a hard disk; student exercises could be turned in electronically; programs could be stored centrally.

Many problems we identified above—incompatible programs, security, cost—apply to a classroom setup. For example, if the key reason for the classroom network is to share software, one must consider that the expense of networking would buy many programs!

Are LANs Really Feasible?

Certainly LANs make sense for some situations. An office with real need for shared data is ripe for networking; a teaching laboratory with thirty machines and a serious requirement for mass storage is a real candidate; local users with infrequent need for an expensive peripheral might consider sharing it.

But our advice on local area networks is guarded. On the whole, the available LANs are brand new systems as of early 1984. Although most of them work, they have many bugs and they usually work on only one or two brands of machines. A campus should use extreme caution in buying an LAN. If you think one is needed then *insist that it be installed and working for a test period before you accept it.* "Kick the tires," don't just rely on promises.

If you are considering a local area network, read the August and November 1983 editions of *PC Magazine,* which have extensive articles on local area networks.

HOST/MICRO NETWORKS

Local area networks are simply a cluster of microcomputers wired together. Often, however, the need is for a different kind of network—linking microcomputers to a "host" minicomputer or mainframe. Examples: An administrator working on a microcomputer needs large student records which are kept on the college mainframe. A sociologist who has a microcomputer in his office wants to run a huge statistical analysis that only a mainframe can handle. An engineer who uses a microcomputer for most problems must go to the mainframe for some special graphics. In many similar cases a link between the micro and the host mainframe is desirable.

Reasons for Host/Micro Networking

Here are a few reasons why linkages between a large host computer and small micros might be useful.

1. *Emulating a terminal, the microcomputer can operate the host.* Of course, this is the standard procedure that has been operating on time-share systems for years. In the examples above (about the administrator, sociologist, and engineer) the people wanted to use the micro simply to operate the mainframe. Either by a modem (a device for linkage over the phone lines) or by hard wires, the microcomputer can connect to many larger computers.

However, in this mode the user must know the software and operational protocols of the larger machine—the software for the micro usually will not work on the mainframe. This means that the user will have to know two programs (one for the micro and one for the mainframe) for all the software he or she wants to use—two word processors, two data base managers, two spreadsheets, etc.

2. *Electronic mail.* We mentioned that electronic mail was a feature of LANs, and the same is true for host/micro combinations. In addition, if the host has both micros and dumb terminals on the network, they can all participate in the electronic mail net.

3. *Access to the host's mass storage and files.* Again, just as with the LANs, the network provides many users with access to the same files.

Users can access files and even move some down to the microcomputer for storage, but they usually cannot use the same software at both ends. This creates a serious problem of duplicated effort. And be warned:

file transfer is not always easy even if you are willing to tolerate two software sets.

4. *Access to expensive and/or specialized peripherals is facilitated by a host/micro network.* Suppose you need a laser-printer, or a super graphics plotter, or some other specialized peripheral? The host is more likely to have that equipment.

However, the cost of maintaining and providing those peripherals will be passed along to you in the charges for using the host computer.

Confusion about Connecting Microcomputers to Larger Machines

Some people think you cannot connect microcomputers to larger machines at all, while others think that the connection is easy and complete. The truth lies somewhere in between. Currently, most microcomputers can be connected to larger computers and simply be used as dumb terminals. That is, the microcomputer simply acts like any other terminal and drives the mainframe. Of course, this capacity alone is an important advantage. But in the process the micro loses all of its stand-alone characteristics as a microcomputer.

Table 10-1 shows various connections between terminals, microcomputers, and larger machines. The chart has four stages, beginning with the simple dumb terminal and moving up to what we call "full interaction networking."

1. *Dumb Terminal Mode:* One way to have distributed access to a mainframe is simply to use a dumb terminal. In this case, the terminal itself has no "brains" or any other peripherals. The terminal simply operates the mainframe and has little or no independent functioning capability.

2. *Micro Emulating Terminal:* A microcomputer can link up to a larger machine and act like a dumb terminal. When functioning as a terminal, it also has no independent capabilities; it is simply driving the mainframe. However, it can be disconnected and used as an independent microcomputer. It has its own brains, can store its own files, and drive its own peripherals. This gives the microcomputer substantial independence over the dumb terminal.

3. *File Transfer Capability:* At a more sophisticated level, the microcomputer can be hooked up to a mainframe, act as a terminal, but also have the added capability of transferring files back and forth between the microcomputer storage system and the mainframe. Unfortunately, this is a fairly complex process. But if your microcomputer and your mainframe are configured properly, it can be done. When files are transferred, however, the microcomputer is likely to have a completely different set of software than the mainframe. You will have to learn to operate both the microcomputer and the mainframe with totally separate software.

4. *Full-Interaction Networking:* The most sophisticated stage would be to have a microcomputer linked to a mainframe, be able to transfer files back and forth, and be able to use the exact same software at both ends. This would be a serious step forward, because the user would have to learn only one set of software and it would be useful at both ends.

Campuses will vary considerably on the capabilities of their networks. Most campuses will have many examples of stage one, the connection of dumb terminals to mainframe. In addition, stage two, the connection of a microcomputer to act as a terminal, is relatively common. However, stage three is still rare, and stage four is even less common. There are very few microcomputers capable of "full interaction networking." The Professional 350 microcomputer series from Digital Equipment Company is one example. The Professional will network with the PDP-11 minicomputer series, using the exact same software at both ends. One reason why we rate DEC microcomputers highly is that Digital appears to be among the leaders in achieving full networking capability.

TABLE 10-1. HOST/MICRO NETWORKING

Name	Terminal	Micro Emulating Terminal	File Transfer	Full Interaction
Host	Main	Main	Main	Main
Station	Terminal	Micro	Micro	Micro
Connection	yes	yes	yes	yes
Station control host	yes	yes	yes	yes
Independent station "brain"	no	yes	yes	yes
Independent station software	no	yes	yes	yes
Independent station work	no	yes	yes	yes
Station can transfer files	no	no	yes	yes
Station can independently use same software as host	no	no	no	yes

Since this is obviously a major thrust for the future, and since we have repeatedly stressed the need for upward growth and sophistication, this networking capacity makes DEC's equipment seem very attractive. Undoubtedly, other manufacturers will strive to accomplish full networking capability in the future.

As this book goes to press, DEC has just announced the new MicroVax, and IBM has announced the new XT/370, two micros that are supposed to do stage four's "full interaction" with the respective companies' mini/mainframe computers. But these machines are expensive—$10,000 and up. The age of full host/micro networking may be here but it looks costly for the moment.

Questions and Answers about Host/Micro Networks

Question: Will most microcomputers act as terminals on a larger host? *Answer:* To some extent most will. The more sophisticated micros will do a much better job.

Question: How do I make the connection between a micro and a host? *Answer:* Either with a hard wire or a modem over a telephone wire.

Question: Can I transfer files from the host to the micro, and *vice versa? Answer:* This is a technical question that only the people who manage your large host will be able to answer.

Question: Can I use the same software on the host and the micro? *Answer:* Probably not, at least not on anything except the top-of-the-line DEC and IBM microcomputers, the $10,000+ range equipment such as the MicroVax and the XT/370.

Question: You mean I must learn two separate sets of software, for the micro and for the large host? *Answer:* Sad, but true.

Question: Suppose I have a big data base on the host mainframe and I want to play with it using my micro? What can I do if the software isn't the same on both ends? Is it hopeless? *Answer:* By no means. You simply switch to terminal mode and use the mainframe. Remember, that is one of the advantages you have with the host/micro linkage—the ability to maximize the strength of both worlds. Frankly, the host will be better at that particular problem than the micro. We are constantly touting the virtues of micros, but to be honest the host can do some things better, and you ought to know when to switch to the host's advantages. As of now, for massive data bases the mainframe is the best solution.

MICROS LINKING WITH INFORMATION NETS

One useful network is the ability to access large national data bases on specialized subjects. Do you want a huge bibliographic search for a research project? Or do you need the latest stockmarket quotations?

Then link your modem to your phone and call the Rockwell Information Network, or the Source, or the Dow Jones News and Retrieval Service, or Compuserve Information Network. These are national data bases on specialized topics. You can dial these and obtain information for a small service charge.

The technical purists are going to fault us here, arguing that the information nets are nothing more than specialized forms of the host/micro network. And technically the purists are right. But remember, this is a book written for *users* not for purists. For the user, access to these large national data bases will seem to be a rather different enterprise than linking up to the local campus mainframe. So we separate this information net function as a special kind of network from the user's perspective.

If you are interested in these services contact any local computer store and talk to them about the various options. In the box on pp. 146-147 we list a few information nets that may be of particular interest to educators.

NATIONAL ELECTRONIC MAIL NETWORKS ENHANCE COMMUNICATION FOR EDUCATORS

Electronic bulletin boards can provide an effective means for communication between teachers, parents, researchers, and others interested in education to interact with and learn from one another. Several emerging networks can provide this service.

MAILNET

One campus electronic mail network, called MAILNET, has recently been established by EDUCOM of Princeton, N.J. This international electronic mail system allows scholars, researchers, and administrators within sixteen participating institutions to shuttle messages instantaneously between computer terminals. This system will allow informal communication between scholars for about 25 cents per single-typed page.

Ed Tech People's Message System

The Department of Educational Technology at San Diego State University established the *Ed Tech PMS* (People's Message System) in November 1982. Since then, reports educational technology professor Bernard Dodge, calls have come in from people in thirty different states. Callers can use the system to share information about education, ask and answer questions, announce new products, and publicize upcoming classes and conferences. Soon, there will also be files of education-related information for users to download onto their systems.

The Ed Tech PMS operates between the hours of 4:30 P.M. and 8:00 A.M. on weekdays and twenty-four hours a day on weekends. The access number is (619) 265-3428.

The Living BBS

San Francisco's Living BBS, cosponsored by Computer Using Educators and Far West Regional Educational laboratory, is another education-centered bulletin board. Its tree-structured format gives organization to the system and encourages dialogue among users. It also promotes a feeling of immediacy and connectedness with real people on the other end of the line. Because of the tree structure, it's easy to follow the course of a discussion that has been going on over time. A password system enables users to send and receive private messages. The Living BBS can be reached twenty-four hours a day, seven days a week. To log on, dial (415) 565-3037.

The Leprechaun

The Leprechaun is an electronic bulletin board supported by the University of Notre Dame. Provided by the office of the assistant provost for computing and the Byteing Irish (the Apple user group at the university), this new board is intended to provide members of the academic community with a means of communicating with one another about computers in education. It features an Apple tips board and help commands that guide new users as they learn about the system. Users can send messages to one another privately by using a password system, and it's also possible to download certain information and programs. The Leprechaun can be reached twenty-four hours a day, seven days a week. To hook up, dial (219) 239-5875.

Education-80

Connecticut's Education-80 was set up "to permit free exchange of information and to allow dialogue about the uses of computers in education." System organization is logical and instructions to new users are clear and straightforward. You can make connections twenty-four hours a day, every day, by calling (203) 629-4375.

SUMMARY

Networks have a future in campus computing. One style, host/micro linkage, is already common and will grow rapidly. The other major style, the local area network (LAN), is still having growing pains and a campus should be cautious in approaching it. Be sure you really need it before you buy one, and then make sure it works with your equipment. Judge by seeing it function at your site, not by promises that the salesman makes.

We close out this chapter with a glossary of common networking terminology. The glossary will be helpful as a review of the main concepts.

A GLOSSARY OF NETWORKING TERMINOLOGY

LAN. A local area network with several microcomputers linked together, usually with shared peripherals such as printer and hard disk drive.

Network user. A station that uses the resources of the network, for example, a microcomputer with only a floppy disk and no printer of its own.

Network server. A device or microcomputer that provides resources to the network, controlling the peripherals and directing traffic in the network. There are two types of servers, "dedicated" (functions only as server) and "shared" (can also serve as an independent microcomputer). Unfortunately, many systems require dedicated servers.

File server. A server that controls files only.

Print server. A server that controls printers. File and print servers can be combined.

Node. Any connection to the network, whether computer or peripheral.

Print spooling. A system that stores information for printing so it can be processed later. This allows a user to send information and then go about his business even if a lineup is blocking the printer. The spooler will print the document when the printer has time.

Topology. The physical shape of the network. There are three types: *star,* with all nodes connected to a central location; *ring,* with all nodes on a closed circle that passes information without going to a central location; and *bus,* with all nodes connected to a linking wire that does not close in a circle. Bus is probably the most common configuration.

Host/Micro network. A large computer with several microcomputers linked to it.

Electronic mail. A communication system that sends information between nodes on the network, working with either LANs or a host/micro setup.

APPENDIX A

A PERSONAL COMPUTER

USER'S GLOSSARY

Applications program. A program created for a specific purpose such as data base management or graphics. Also called applications software.

Arithmetic logic unit. Part of the CPU that is responsible for actually processing or manipulating the data by performing arithmetic computations or logical operations.

Assembly language. A means of communicating with the computer by using mnenonics to represent machine operations.

Backup. A spare copy of software or data in the event of damage or accidental erasure of the original copy.

BASIC. Beginners All Purpose Instruction Code. An easy-to-learn, high-level language popular for small computers.

Batch processing. A method of gathering and transcribing source data as a group. The input records are then processed in a batch by some computer program.

Baud. A measure of the speed at which computer information travels, loosely, bits per second.

Binary numbers. A numbering system including only ones and zeros; an efficient way to store information in a computer because the hundreds of thousands of microscopic switches in a computer can only be "1," on, or "0," off.

Bit. An abbreviation of "binary digit," the smallest piece of information recognized by a computer.

Boot. To start up a program.

Buffer. A device used to resolve differences between pieces of equipment, i.e., computer and printer, that operate at incompatible speeds.

Bug. A defect or error in either the hardware or the software program.

Byte. Eight adjacent bits that represent one numeric or alphabetic character, or symbol.

Cathode-ray tube (CRT). A televisionlike picture tube used with most small computers to display text.

149

Central Processing Unit (CPU). The brain of the computer consisting of the arithmetic-logic unit, control unit, and primary storage. The CPU directs all of the operations in the computer and interprets and executes instructions.

Chip. A single package (also known as an integrated circuit or IC) holding hundreds of thousands of microscopic components. The term is derived from the formed flakes or "chips" of silicon of which they are made.

COBOL (Common Business Oriented Language). A high-level language that was designed to take advantage of the computer's storage capacity for business processing.

Command. A character or word that causes a computer to do something.

Compatibility. The ability of equipment to interface without special adapters or other interceding devices.

Compiler. Software that translates high-level languages (BASIC, COBOL, FORTRAN, PL1) into machine-level language for the computer to use.

Computer. Any device that can store and modify both data and instructions.

Computer-assisted instruction (CAI). Instruction involving interaction between the student and the computer.

Computer network. A series of computers connected to one another to communicate and share information.

Computer program. A collection of instructions to tell the computer to do a specific task or series of tasks.

Control unit. The part of the CPU that is responsible for directing and controlling the activities of the computer.

Courseware. Educational or computer-assisted instruction software.

CPU. See Central Processing Unit.

Cursor. Normally a flashing or nonflashing rectangle on the monitor that indicates where the user's next entry will be placed.

Daisy wheel. Impact printer that uses a rotating type wheel to produce letter-quality text.

Data. A term referring to the information, facts, numbers, letters and symbols produced and/or acted on by a computer.

Data base. A collection of related data retrievable by a computer, such as a mailing list.

Data base management. A software package designed to assist users with varying needs to access and use a data base. In addition to locating particular items within the files, the program must be capable of affecting additions or changes in the information stored.

Debug. Checking a program to remove errors.

Disassembler. A program that translates a computer's native language into assembly language.

Disk (or diskette). A round piece of magnetic-coated material (rigid metal or floppy plastic) used to store data.

Disk drive. A peripheral device that can store or retrieve information onto a disk.

Display. A visual image representing computer information, generally via a CRT or on printed paper.

Documentation. The instruction manual for a piece of hardware or software.

DOS (Disk Operating System). The operating system used in the Apple II.

Dot matrix. A type of printer that uses needles which strike the paper through a ribbon to form characters from a pattern of dots. Low in cost, dot matrix printers produce text that is readable but far below letter quality.

Downtime. Any period of time when the computer is not working or is unavailable.

Ergonomics. Term coined to describe the study of interactions between humans and machines.

Electronic mail. Digital transmissions of messages from one location to another via computer-controlled data communication linkages.

EPROM (Erasable Programmable Read Only Memory). Read only memory that can be erased by exposing the integrated circuit to ultraviolet light.

Firmware. Software permanently placed in memory, usually into read-only memory (ROM).

Floppy disk. A thin, flexible disk of plastic with a magnetic coating used for storing data. They can generally be found in two sizes: $5^1/_4$" and 8".

FORTRAN. FORmula TRANslation. A high-level computer language primarily used for mathematical and scientific applications.

Global search and replace. An editing function in word processing software that allows the user to specify a word or phrase and its desired replacement; the program will search the text for every appearance and automatically make the substitution.

Graphics plotter. Device that can provide multicolored, hard-copy representations of complex graphics.

Hard copy. An actual printout of information from the computer onto paper.

Hard disk. Rigid platter (usually aluminum) used for storing computer data. It may range from $5^1/_4$ to 14 inches in diameter. They are sometimes mounted in a stack on a spindle to increase storage capacity, which is already far in excess of that provided by floppy disks.

Hardware. The physical, mechanical equipment making up the computer system.

High-level language. Any programming language that allows the programmer to give instructions to the computer in English-like text as opposed to the numerical (binary) code.

Initialize. To prepare the disk for data storage (also known as formatting).

Input. The process of transferring data into the computer.

Input/Output (I/O). The two-way exchange of information that goes on between the computer and the peripheral equipment.

Integrated circuit (IC). See Chip.

Integrated software. Software that combines several related application programs within a single package, making it possible to merge information from separate files.

Interactive. A computer system that allows a two-way conversation between the user and the computer.

Interface. Hardware or software used to connect two devices (peripherals and computers) that could not otherwise be connected.

Keyboarding. Entering information via the keyboard.

Kilobyte (K). Approximately one thousand bytes.

Load. To put programs and/or data into a computer.

Large-scale integration (LSI). A method of constructing electronic circuits in such a way that thousands of circuits can be stored on a single silicon chip.

Machine language. The binary-coded, native language of the computer.

Megabyte. Unit used to describe the computer's memory or storage capacity; it represents 1000K.

Memory. That part of the computer that holds data and instructions. The data are held in the form of binary ones and zeros.

Menu. A list of commands presented to the user as options with which to run a program.

Microcomputer. A computer whose CPU is a microprocessor.

Microprocessor. The central processing unit of a computer, usually in a single integrated circuit.

Modem. MOdulator-DEModulator (also known as a data set), a device that allows computers to communicate over phone lines by converting the digital signals into musical tones (modulating) and then back again to digital signals (demodulating).

Monitor. A screen that looks like a television set but is made specifically to be used with a computer.

Mouse. A small rolling device that is used to move text and illustrations on the CRT screen.

Network. An interconnected system of computers and/or terminals (also called nodes).

Node. A station in a network; a node is either a computer or a terminal.

Operating system. Software that controls or oversees the operation of the computer system. This software acts as an intermediary between the hardware and the applications software. Examples: DOS = Disk

Operating System; SOS = Sophisticated Operating System; CP/M = Control Program/Microcomputer.

Pascal. A high-level programming language.

Peripheral. A device, usually hardware, that is external but connected to the computer. Popular peripherals are printers and disk drives.

Personal computer. A general-purpose microcomputer small enough to transport without much difficulty and inexpensive enough to be owned by an individual.

Primary storage. The location area in the computer where all input and output are stored while waiting to be sent to other locations.

Printer. An output device that produces a printed copy of the information from the computer. One of the most popular printers is the letter-quality printer, which produces documents of typewriter quality or better.

Printout. Copy produced by the printer.

Processing programs. Programs that are used to simplify program preparation and execution, e.g., compiler, assemblers, and interpreters.

Program. (a) To prepare a set of instructions for the computer; (b) a set of instructions that tell the computer to perform a specific task.

PROM (Programmable Read Only Memory). Allows the user or manufacturer to program or hardwire instructions one time into memory, after which it cannot be changed.

Random Access Memory (RAM). Memory that has both read and write capabilities. The contents in RAM are volatile, that is when the computer is turned off the data stored in RAM are lost.

RF modulator (or modulator). The device that allows any ordinary television set to be used as an output device or monitor for the computer.

ROM (Read Only Memory). The area of memory that cannot be altered by the user. Contains the firmware placed in memory at the point of manufacture.

Simulation. A representation by the computer of something in action.

Software. Generic name for all computer programs.

Software house. A company that produces and/or provides programs and support services to users.

SOS (Sophisticated Operating System). The operating system used with the Apple III.

System software. Software that performs all data transfers and hardware manipulations required by the micro's physical components.

Tape drive. A device that converts information stored on magnetic tape into impulses that will be accepted by a computer.

Telecommunication. The transmission/reception between terminals or between terminals and computers over phone lines, satellites, radio waves, etc.

Terminal. An input/output device used for two-way communication with a computer. It generally includes a keyboard, CRT, and printer.

Timesharing. The sharing of both power and cost of a large computer facility by a number of users via terminals.

Track. A section of a disk or tape.

User friendly. A term referring to software that is easy to use and understand due to clear instructions.

Users' group. A support group or organization made up of computer users who meet to share knowledge regarding their software and hardware.

Very high level languages. Nonprocedural languages such as FOCUS and RAMUS that are moving away from procedural step-by-step instructions required in languages such as BASIC and FORTRAN.

APPENDIX B

FUTURE EDUCATIONAL

DEVELOPMENTS:

INTERACTIVE VIDEO

INTERACTIVE VIDEO: AN EXAMPLE

Your son is graduating from high school and is perplexed about his future. He stops by the career guidance center and takes a shiny metallic disk the size of a phonograph record labeled "Careers" off the shelf. He proceeds to insert it into a briefcase-sized device and relaxes in front of a television with a small hand-held remote control. The screen comes alive. A familiar celebrity welcomes the boy, after which a series of questions are asked:

Would you:
1. like to seek a job?
2. prefer to attend a trade school?
3. like to attend a college or university?

He presses #3 on his remote control. The celebrity acknowledges the boy's choice and briefly highlights several advantages of higher education.

The speaker concludes by asking your son what major interests he has. After responding, the boy is asked what geographic location he prefers. Not wanting to pay out-of-state tuition, he types in the abbreviation for his home state, California. The celebrity mentions that several universities in California offer extensive programs in his chosen field of "Natural Resource Management." Seeking more specific information, the TV screen presents a list of possible locations. Choosing Pebble Beach State University results in a short "travel log type" audio-visual presentation of the school and surrounding points of interest. Continued response to questioning provides the hopeful student with visual segments including the building in his major field, a tour of the facilities by the dean,

155

photos of the dormitories and off campus housing alternatives . . . in fact, any information the student desires.

This scenario is not a futuristic dream. With the technology of interactive video this "diagnostic branching" example can be accomplished today. In fact, today your son could be at the instructional media center selecting a few disks to take for the weekend, one on biology 2A and another called "Introduction to Abnormal Psychology." He places the courseware in his small backpack with his personal learning system, a standard three-ring binder. On Saturday, after jogging along the sand, he spreads out his beach towel and opens the cover to his binder. A flat television screen is exposed. He inserts a disk and a Pulitzer Prize winning biologist appears on the screen. Studying on the beach begins. Again, the technology of solar or battery powered laser disk, flat screen TV, and voice synthesis can accomplish this form of interactive video training today.

WHAT IS INTERACTIVE VIDEO?

Interactive video (I/V) is a system combining the best of two technologies, Computer-Assisted Instruction (CAI) and Closed Circuit Television (CCTV).

A brief explanation of CAI and CCTV will reveal how the term "interactive" is used in this context. CAI uses the computer's ability to store large amounts of data (text, graphics, etc.) that can be "randomly accessed" to aid the *individual* learner as he seeks information. For example, a straightforward approach to learning might be reading a book from first page to last, listening to a lecture from beginning to end, or watching a training film from start to finish. The learner "passively receives" knowledge in each of these "linear" one-way approaches.

Contrast this with the efficient reader who learns to skim the book rapidly, read main headings, introductions, and conclusions, and access chapters or segments of interest in any order. In reading a book most people "interact" by "randomly accessing" those segments of information pertinent to their needs. Using this strategy the reader has control over the text he reads. Books are simply another type of data base, a storage medium for text.

With lectures and films, however, an individual trying to interact with the speaker could be disruptive to the audience. Few students would ask the projectionist to back up or skip ahead to personally relevant topics. Unfortunately, individuals have less control over the information they receive in groups.

A simple application illustrating the computer's use in CAI is in teaching and testing. In this application the computer interacts with the student via a terminal (keyboard and monitor) by asking questions to determine if the presentation was understood. If not, the student is presented with more fundamentals to furnish the necessary prerequisite knowledge. If the computer's presentation is too basic, it will branch to higher-level lessons commensurate with the student's ability.

In the usual configuration, the computer accesses information in the form of booklike text, graphs, charts, or even animation. Why not access information segments presented by the most popular source—another human being?

Thus, we arrive at prerecorded video in which the same message can be recorded on a single videotape or video disk using several languages and multiple levels of complexity to target different audiences. Interactive video uses a microprocessor or computer to access only those video segments that meet the user's needs. I/V finds useful applications in training, procedure demonstration, and as a storage and retrieval system for visual images.

In summary, an effective interactive training program contains information relevant to a broad range of student interests and skill levels. Information is embedded in the data storage medium (videotape, videodisk, computer disk, etc.) in a hierarchical fashion. The "intelligent" program pretests the user to determine which level of subject complexity is appropriate. With each student response, the program further guides the user along the path reflecting the student's most immediate information needs. Based on the learner's responses, he may be returned to review remedial information, branched to higher or lower levels of complexity, or bumped ahead to new information resulting in mastery learning at the most efficient rate for each individual.

USES OF INTERACTIVE VIDEO

To date, I/V is found highly effective in at least three somewhat overlapping areas: instruction/training, presentations, and cataloguing.

Instruction/Training
A widely used application for interactive video is in training and instruction. Interactive video becomes a perfect medium for instructional situations involving: (1) diagnostic branching; (2) CAI; and (3) simulations or representations involving human behavior.

Diagnostic branching could, for example, replace on a single diskette the information found on a shelf full of trouble-shooting guides for automotive repair or volumes of medical diagnostic journals.

With complex electronic equipment, for instance, an I/V user can point to a portion of a still frame on a touch-sensitive video monitor and see that section expanded. By touching screws shown on the screen the learner can see them magically unscrew. Depending upon the program's intent this could be an informative simulated disassembly or a test where precise procedures must be followed.

For the squeamish biology student, dissecting a frog could likewise be done with a touch-sensitive screen. Animal lovers would rejoice at the thought of saving so many amphibious friends. This application becomes more serious when used to document rare human disorders or dangerous equipment. Few students receive the opportunity for "hands on" experience with these rare or costly events. I/V could easily fill this void.

CAI provides streamlined personalized teaching and testing paths necessary for mastery learning. In addition, built-in grading can be incorporated, thus eliminating a time-consuming task for instructors. In business, I/V is a cost-effective method used to train new employees while maintaining continuity through standardized presentations.

For example, *orienting* new students and employees normally requires a learning period lasting weeks or months until they are operating at maximum efficiency. Not only *their* time but also the valuable time of senior faculty and staff are wasted. A well-produced I/V orientation program will provide detailed information specific to each user's needs. More important, this guidance would be available when the newcomer needs it, not just during the first two weeks when the topic may not yet be relevant. For example, an orientation to the library system can be quite complex. By the time a student requires help late in the year, he has already forgotten the details.

Simulations involving human behavior that would be impossible to represent through text or charts can be dramatized—a picture *can* be worth a thousand words. Human behavior is usually too complex to quantify accurately. If a medical text instructs the student to inject 10 cc of interferon at exactly the moment he patient's face turns a flushed red, it is easy to see how qualitative decisions can be misinterpreted. A few seconds of live video could replace pages of detailed descriptions.

I/V is also unique in its ability to document rare events and dramatize possible incidents. No other method can impart the realism and consequences of an incorrect choice so effectively. Whether the instruction is in pilot training as he crashes, in medical training as the patient gasps and dies, or in nuclear physics training as a nuclear plant explodes, the impact will be long lasting. Seeing is believing. When the consequences of error are serious, I/V simulation is easily cost justifiable.

Presentations

The impact, realization, and believability of television lends itself well to human presentations involving motivational messages such as sales, religious, or self-realization topics and "how to" demonstrations of a manual or body-related task such as tying your shoes, booting up a computer, or the steps to an intricate classical dance.

The opening scenario depicted a high school graduate using an interactive video system to facilitate his decision on the university he would attend. The same data base (lasar disk) could also be used to *attract* highly qualified and desirable faculty and staff. Equally important is that students, faculty, and staff who decide on a particular location based on an accurate knowledge of the facilities and environment are more likely to become long-term residents. Thus, the retention rate is increased and costly turnover is reduced.

Cataloguing

Still another adaptation of I/V is using the video disk as an extremely dense storage medium. I/V can accomplish cataloguing and archive retrieval of any visual data, much like microfiche currently attempts to do. Video disk is an especially fast medium for accessing up to 54,000 still frames.

THE FUTURE OF INTERACTIVE VIDEO

In the next few years I/V will be little more than an adolescent, having experienced its infancy in the early 1980s. Growth in educational institutions will be conservative because, while they have the personnel capable of implementing good I/V programs, they generally lack funding. Private enterprise can afford the system but lacks the specialists in instructional design and computer operations. It is estimated that with the accelerated growth rate of computer technology the ability to provide adequate instruction will represent less than 10 percent of the need. The efficiency of I/V will be able to offset this dismal prediction.

Future Technology

Among the more interesting developments will be recordable (read/write) video disks that will allow updating, thus removing the last major drawback to disks. The combination of fast random access with user recording capability will dramatically affect I/V's usefulness.

As with all electronic technologies the trend will continue toward miniaturization, higher capacities, and lower prices. Digitalized compressed audio will allow still frames to be accompanied with longer descriptive narration.

Nation- and worldwide networking will become commonplace, allowing individuals from any geographic location to access large data bases in the public domain. Teleconferencing currently uses live video transmission and allows two or more parties to communicate visually. In the future, it will also be combined with prerecorded information.

Already a reality at Disney World's futuristic Epcot Center in Florida, with major financial institutions following suit, are interactive video disks that provide information to visitors via touch-sensitive TV screens. If, after exhausting the prerecorded centralized data base, the user still has questions, an on-line "live" human host appears on the screen to offer further guidance.

Imagine students efficiently completing the vast majority of their coursework while interacting with the video and computer data bases. Yet, for specific state-of-the-art questions, any student within a statewide university system can access an instructor or research authority doing his "on line" office hours from his beachside veranda.

With this vision of the future, we bring this book to a close. You, the decision maker, must now decide whether to help bring your campus along with the sweeping change.

REFERENCES

AIKEN, ROBERT M. "Computer Science Education in the 1980's." Computer, 13 (1980): 41–46.

AMERICAN ASSOCIATION OF COMMUNITY AND JUNIOR COLLEGES AND ASSOCIATION OF COMMUNITY COLLEGE TRUSTEES. *A Guide to Making Intelligent Computing Decisions.* Washington, D.C.: AACJC, 1980 (ERIC ED 192 840).

ASP, E. H., AND J. GORDON. "Development of a Computer-Assisted Program for Undergraduate Instruction." *Journal of Nutrition Education,* 13 (1981, March Supplement): 91–95.

BILLINGS, KAREN, AND DAVID MOURSAND. *Are You Computer Literate?* Portland, Ore.: Dilithium Press, 1979.

CARBONE, ROBERT. *Presidential Passages.* Washington, D.C.: American Council on Education, 1981.

CAREY, SUSAN. "Carnegie-Mellon Facility Searches for Ways to Use Small Computers in the Liberal Arts." *Wall Street Journal,* June 30, 1983: 46.

CASSEL, DON, AND MARTIN JACKSON. *Introduction to Computers and Information Processing.* Reston, Va.: Reston Publishing Company, 1980.

CHAMBERS, JACK A., AND JERRY W. SPRECHER. "Computer Assisted Instruction: Current Trends and Critical Issues." *Communications of the ACM2,* June 1980: 332–342.

CHRONICLE OF HIGHER EDUCATION. "Free Courses, Workshop; Better Manuals." *Computer Notes: The Chronicle of Higher Education,* June 22, 1983: 22.

COHEN, M. D., AND J. G. MARCH. *Leadership and Ambiguity.* New York: McGraw-Hill, 1974.

COVVEY, H. DOMINIC, AND NEAL H. MCALISTER. *Computer Consciousness: Surviving the Automated 80's.* Reading, Mass.: Addison-Wesley, 1980.

DLABAY, L. R., COMP. "Educator's Guide to Computer Periodicals." Curriculum Review, 21 (May 1982): 144–146.

DOERR, CHRISTINE. *Microcomputers and the 3 R's: A Guide for Teachers.* Rochelle Park, N.J.: Hayden Book Co., 1979.

EMERY, JAMES C. *Planning for Computing in Higher Education*. EDUCOM Series in Computing and Telecommunications in Higher Education, No. 5. Boulder, Colo.: Westview Press, 1980.

FARRELL, CHARLES S. "The Computerization of Carnegie-Mellon." *The Chronicle of Higher Education*, March 1983: 6–7.

FERRARI, MICHAEL. *Profiles of American College Presidents*. Ann Arbor: Michigan State University, 1970.

FLANIGAN, JAMES. "Personal Computer Industry: The Current Shake-Up Is Not a Shakeout." *Los Angeles Times*, Business Section, Sept. 21, 1983: 1.

FRIEDLANDER, JACK. "Institutional Practices of Part-Time Faculty." In *Using Part-Time Faculty Effectively*, Michael H. Parsons (ed.). San Francisco: Jossey-Bass, 1980.

GILLESPIE, ROBERT G. "Goals for Computing in Higher Education." *Journal of Educational Technology System*, 9 (1981): 171–178.

HAMBLEN, J., AND T. BAIRD. *Fourth Inventory: Computers in Higher Education*. Princeton, N.J.: EDUCOM, 1979.

HAMBLEN, JOHN W. *Computer Literacy and Societal Impact of Computers: Education and Manpower*. St. James, Mo.: October 1978 (ERIC ED 178 049).

HARRIS, KATHRYN. "Coleco Again Unable to Ship New Computer," *Los Angeles Times*, Business Section, Sept. 21, 1983: 1.

HENDERSON, DONALD L. "Educational Uses of the Computer: Implications for Teacher/Administrator Training." *Educational Technology*, 18 (August 1978): 41–42.

HOFFMAN, LANCE J., ED. *Computers and Privacy in the Next Decade*. New York: Academic Press, 1980.

JOHNSON, DAVID C., RONALD E. ANDERSON, THOMAS P. HANSEN, AND DANIEL L. KLASSEN. "Computer Literacy—What Is It?" *Mathematics Teacher*, 73 (February 1980): 91–96.

KATZ, MARTIN R. *SIGI Information Bulletin*. Princeton, N.J.: Educational Testing Service, 1981.

KATZAN JR., HARRY. *Office Automation: A Manager's Guide*. New York: American Management Association, 1982.

KLASSEN, DANIEL L., RONALD E. ANDERSON, THOMAS P. HANSEN, AND DAVID C. JOHNSON. *A Study of Computer Use and Literacy in Science Education, Final Report 1978–1980*. Minneapolis: Minnesota Education Computing Consortium, 1980.

KLEIN, WALTER VON, CHARLES R. THOMAS, AND ROBERT A. NETTER. "Administrative Application of Computers: What Now?" *College and University*, 5 (Summer 1979): 339–340.

KOLLER, WILLIAM. *Your Career in Computer-Related Occupations*. New York: Arco Publishing, 1979.

KRIEGER, M, AND F. PACK. "Unix as an Application Environment." *Byte*, October 1983: 209–210.

KULIK, J. A., R. L. BANGERT, AND G. W. WILLIAMS. "Effects of Computer Based Teaching on Secondary School Students." *Journal of Educational Psychology*, Vol. 75, No. 1 (1983): 19–26.

KULIK, J. A., C. C. KULIK, AND P. A. COHEN. "Effectiveness of Computer Based College Teaching: A Meta-Analysis of Findings." *Review of Educational Research,* Vol. 50, No. 4 (Winter 1980): 525–544.

LAURIE, EDWARD J. *Computers, Automation, and Society.* Homewood, Ill.: Richard D. Irwin, 1979.

LESLIE, DAVID W., SAMUEL E. KELLAMS, AND G. MANNY GUNNE. *Part-Time Faculty in American Higher Education.* New York: Praeger, 1982.

LEVENTHAL, LANCE A., AND IRVIN STAFFORD. *Why Do You Need a Personal Computer?* New York: John Wiley and Sons, 1981.

LEWIS, R., AND E. D. TAGG. *Computer Assisted Learning: Scope, Progress, and Limits.* London: Heinemann Educational Books, 1980.

LYON, BECHY J. *Mind Transplants, or: The Role of Computer Assisted Instruction in the Future of the Library.* Paper. Bethesda, Md.: Lister Hill National Center for Biomedical Communications, 1975 (ERIC ED 108 674).

MAGARRELL, J. "Computer Literacy Gaining Place in Undergraduate Curriculum." *Chronicle of Higher Education,* 24, No. 8 (April 21, 1982): 1, 8 (a).

MAGARRELL, J. "Two Colleges Plan to Equip All Students with Computers." *The Chronicle of Higher Education,* 25, No. 9 (October 27, 1982): 2 (b).

MAGARRELL, J. "Student and Staff Discounts; Insider Trustees." *The Chronicle of Higher Education,* 25, No. 17 (January 5, 1983): 25 (c).

MAGARRELL, J. "Stanford Professors Computing at Home." *The Chronicle of Higher Education,* 25, No. 22 (February 9, 1983): 27 (d).

MAGARRELL, J. "College Students Said to Require $1 Billion a Year for Computing." *The Chronicle of Higher Education,* 26, No. 1 (March 2, 1983): 1, 6 (e).

MAGARRELL, J. "How Faculty Members Use Microcomputers." *The Chronicle of Higher Education,* 26, No. 1 (March 2, 1983): 10 (f).

MAGARRELL, J. "Microcomputers Proliferate on College Campuses." *The Chronicle of Higher Education,* 26, No. 6 (April 6, 1983): 9 (g).

MAGARRELL, J. "3,000 Apples at Drexel University; Upgrade at Stevens Tech." *The Chronicle of Higher Education,* 26, No. 9 (April 27, 1983): 19–20 (h).

MANDEL, STEVEN L. *Computers and Data Processing Today with Pascal.* St. Paul, Minn.: 1983.

McCREDIE, JOHN W. (ED). *Campus Computing Strategies.* Bedford, Mass.: Digital Press, 1983.

McDONALD, KIM. "Students Required to Buy Computers." *The Chronicle of Higher Education,* 25, No. 1 (Sept. 1, 1982): 3.

McGLYNN, DANIEL R. *Personal Computer, Home, Professional, and Small Business Applications.* New York: John Wiley and Sons, 1979.

NATIONAL SCIENCE FOUNDATION. *Process of Technological Innovation: Reviewing the Literature.* Washington, D.C.: National Science Foundation, 1983.

OFFICE OF TECHNOLOGY ASSESSMENT. "Information Technology and Its Impact on American Education." Report: Summer 1982.

OLIVIERI, PETER, AND MICHAEL W. RUBIN. *Computers and Programming: A Neoclassical Approach.* New York: McGraw-Hill, 1975.

OSBORNE, ADAM. *An Introduction to Microcomputers.* . New York: Osborne/McGraw-Hill, 1980.

PARSONS, M. H. *Using Part-Time Faculty Effectively.* San Francisco: Jossey-Bass, 1980.

PORAT, M. A. *The Information Economy.* Washington D.C.: United States Department of Commerce, Office of Telecommunications, 1977.

REED, SALLEY. "Plugging Teachers into Computer Era." *New York Times Book Review,* 12 (April 24, 1983): 44.

ROGERS, MICHAEL. "Trouble in Computerland." *Newsweek,* Sept. 26, 1983: 72–74.

SAAL, HARRY. "Local Area Networks." *Byte,* May 1983: 60–70.

SCHWARTZ, H. J. "Monsters and Mentors: Computer Applications for Humanistic Education." *College English,* 44 (February 1982): 141–152.

SILVER, GERALD A. *The Social Impact of Computers.* New York: Harcourt, Brace Jovanovich, 1979.

STRANGE, J. H. "Adapting to the Computer Revolution." *Current Issues in Higher Education Annual Series,* 5 (1981): 14–18.

SUMMER, CLAIRE, AND WALTER A. LEVY, EDS. *The Affordable Computer: Microcomputer Applications in Business and Industry.* New York: Amacom, 1979.

TURNER, JUDITH AXLER. "Colorado Professors to Get 1,000." *The Chronicle of Higher Education,* 26, No. 12 (May 18, 1983): 28.

U.S. DEPARTMENT OF HEALTH, EDUCATION, AND WELFARE. *Records, Computers, and the Rights of Citizens: Report of the Secretary's Advisory Committee on Automated Personal Data Systems.* Boston: MIT Press, 1973.

VARVEN, JEAN. "The Schoolhouse Apple." *Softalk,* 1983: 115.

VLES, JOSEPH. *Computer Fundamentals for Nonspecialists.* New York: Amacon, 1980.

WINKLER, KAREN J. "Interest in Computer Literacy Set Off Big Textbook Boom" *The Chronicle of Higher Education,* 25, No. 2 (Sept. 8, 1982): 1, 21.

WINTER, PATTY. *The Apple Guide to Personal Computers in Education.* Cupertino: Apple Computer, 1983.

INDEX

INDEX

A

Access to machines, 16–17, 85–86
Accounting, 49, 113, 117
ACM Sigcue Bulletin, 132
Adam computer, 41
Administrative applications, 7, 48
American College Testing Service, 125
Apple Computer Company, 27, 38–42, 45, 47, 51, 52, 64, 68, 79, 89
   Lisa, 29, 30, 39, 42, 45–47, 69–71, 81
   MacIntosh, 70, 71, 76–77, 81
   II, 29, 38, 39, 45, 61, 69–71, 130
   IIe, 29, 39, 40, 61, 62, 69, 72, 81, 91–93
   II Plus, 120
   III, 29, 39, 40, 42, 45, 61, 62, 69–71
Apple Education News, 132
Applications software, 45–48, 114–115
Arithmetic/logic unit (ALU), 30, 32
Atari, 39, 79–80
   400, 130
   800, 120
Atari Institute, 2
Audio-visual equipment, 4
Authoring languages, 121–122

B

Baird, T., 13
Baldridge, J. Victor, 104
Bangert, R. L., 123
Bar-code readers, 32
BASIC, 113
Batch processing, 4
Book, The (Apple Computer Company), 129–130
Brown University, 5, 86, 96
Budget spreadsheets, 105, 107
Business graphics, 49

C

Cable television, 1
California Institute of Technology, 109
California Software Evaluation Forum, 130
California State University at Long Beach (CSULB), 109–110
CAN, 7
Career guidance, 125–128
Carey, Susan, 136
Carnegie-Mellon University, 19, 21–25, 72, 86, 109, 136–137
Central processing unit (CPU), 29, 30, 32, 66

167